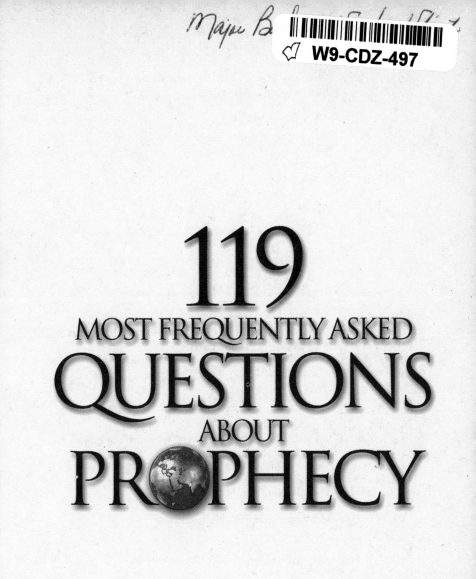

119

MOST FREQUENTLY ASKED

QUESTIONS

ABOUT

PROPHECY

119 Most Frequently Asked Questions About Prophecy
Copyright ©2003 by Midnight Call Ministries
Published by The Olive Press, a subsidiary of Midnight Call, Inc.
Columbia, South Carolina, 29228

Copy Typist:	Lynn Jeffcoat
Copy Editor:	Susanna Cancassi
Proofreaders:	Angie Peters, Susanna Cancassi
Layout/Design:	Michelle Kim
Lithography:	Simon Froese
Cover Design:	Michelle Kim

Library of Congress Cataloging-in-Publication Data

Froese, Arno
119 Most Frequently Asked Questions About Prophecy
ISBN #0-937422-58-4

1. Prophecy
2. Biblical Teaching

Printed in the United States of America

The sole purpose of publishing this book is to encourage the reader to surrender and consecrate his life to Jesus Christ.

All funds received from the sale of this book will be used exclusively to further the Gospel.

No one associated with this ministry receives a royalty for any of the literature published by The Olive Press.

CONTENTS

- Did God create the world or did it randomly evolve over a period of millions of years?

- If God did create the world, then why is it imperfect?

- Why did God allow sin into the world?

- If man started out sinless, then how did sin originate?

- How did God intend to redeem man and save him from his sin?

The People of Salvation

Jerusalem and the Temple

- How many times has the Temple been built and destroyed?

- Can the Jews reinstitute Temple service without the Ark of the Covenant?

- Where is the Ark of the Covenant?

- If the Temple sacrifices only acted as a sin "covering," and Jesus' blood is the power for the remission of sins, then why would Temple sacrifices need to be reinstituted?

- Why is it necessary for the Temple to exist during the Millennium, described in Ezekiel 40-48?

- Are any preparations to rebuild the Temple taking place now?

- Is it possible for the new Temple to be built in our days?

- If the new Temple will be used by the Antichrist, can't it be built beside the Dome of the Rock?

- Is Jerusalem Jewish or international?

- Will peace come to Israel?

Chapter **4** **57**

The Church

- There are literally thousands of denominations; how can we identify the true Church?

- How can I recognize the true Church?

- Will Jesus bring peace?

- Why is this false gospel so successful?

- Will Christians experience persecution?

- How can we recognize deception?

- What is "another" Gospel?

- What is the future of the Church?

- What is the difference between the Body of Christ and the Bride of Christ?

- Are there two Second Comings?

- What's the difference between the Rapture and the Second Coming?

- When will the Rapture take place?

- Can you biblically support your stand on the Pre-Trib Rapture?

- What will happen after the Rapture occurs?

Daniel's Prophecy

- Why would the Antichrist take away the daily sacrifice?

- How does Nebuchadnezzar's image relate to our days?

- Does the handwriting on the wall in Daniel chapter 5 have any prophetic significance for the endtimes?

- What are the historical dates of Daniel's 70th week showing that the birth and death of the Messiah has already taken place precisely as prophesied by Daniel?

- What book was Daniel instructed to seal?

The Antichrist

- Who is Antichrist?
- Will the Antichrist be a Jew?
- Why hasn't the Antichrist been revealed yet?

- The Antichrist is the first beast mentioned in Revelation 13 and the false prophet is the second beast. To whom does the mark belong?
- Is there more than one Antichrist?
- When will the Antichrist be revealed?
- How can we recognize the spirit of the Antichrist?

The Nations

- Which nations play a major endtime role?
- What is the intention of the nations?
- What does God think about the nations of the world?
- Why is Rome so significant?
- Will Rome be the capital of the New World Order?
- Will Rome be the capital of Europe?

The New World Order

- How new is the New World Order?
- Will the New World Order replace a nation's sovereignty?
- How does the New World Order relate to the United Nations?
- Who rules the United Nations?

Chapter 14   155

Revelation Events

The Millennium

- What is the Millennium?
- What is the cause of the Millennium?
- Who will take part in the Millennium?
- Where will the Church be during the Millennium?
- Will mortal saints intermingle on earth with the immortal during the Millennium?
- What is the last battle according to Scripture?
- What is the aim of Gog and Magog?
- What will happen to the unbeliever after the Millennium?
- Can you explain the heavenly Jerusalem?
- What will our position be after the Millennium?

INTRODUCTION

The outline of this book came to me on a flight to India. I was scheduled to speak at a number of locations about Bible prophecy, specifically highlighting its fulfillment. During these engagements, it became increasingly clear that a majority of today's believers fail to understand the principles of prophetic Scripture; subsequently, they shy away from studying this important part of God's Word. Since prophecy makes up approximately 25–30% of Scripture, it is rather unfortunate that many Christians are missing a specific blessing that God has promised to those who hear and read the prophetic Word: "Blessed is he that readeth, and they that hear the words of this prophecy, and keep those things which are written therein: for the time is at hand" (Revelation 1:3). The pages that follow are my attempt to present clear, simple answers to the fundamental subject of Christ's return and its relationship to our time. It is my prayer that both the questions and answers printed in this book relating to the Rapture, the Second Coming of Christ, Israel and the Gentile world will help Christians to better understand Bible prophecy.

I have based my answers on Scripture to the best of my

ability. My answers, of course, are not the final authority, nor are they conclusive, because the Bible says that we only "know in part." It is only those subjects of which I am certain that I have presented in this book.

I pray that this work not only contributes to a better understanding of eschatology, but that it also moves the reader to increase his own study of the Scripture, thereby fulfilling Paul's prayer for the Corinthians, "So that ye come behind in no gift; waiting for the coming of our Lord Jesus Christ" (1st Corinthians 1:7).

CHAPTER 1

CREATION

 Did God create the world or did it randomly evolve over a period of millions of years?

 The Holy Spirit inspired the Apostle Paul to write these words: "Because that which may be known of God is manifest in them; for God hath shewed it unto them. For the invisible things of him from the creation of the world are clearly seen, being understood by the things that are made, even his eternal power and God-head; so that they are without excuse" (Romans 1:19–20). Based on the visible world around us and all that it contains, we can conclude that this world did not come into existence as the result of an "accident." On the contrary, it was a perfectly designed, divinely orchestrated event that was completed in six days, not several million years.

The argument between creationists and evolutionists continues: Scientists try to prove that the world and all life forms evolved, while Christians use the same fundamental approach to prove that God created the world. But our final authority is Scripture, which says, "Through faith we understand that the worlds were framed by the word of God, so that things which are seen were not made of things which do appear" (Hebrews 11:3). Notice the use of the pronoun "we" instead of "they." For the believer, it is eternally settled in heaven: "In the beginning God created the heaven and the earth." We fully comprehend this fact by faith!

 If God did create the world, then why is it imperfect?

 The world exists in a state of imperfection as the result of sin. Not only does the Bible clearly teach that man is imperfect; but every scientist, anthropologist, historian, psychologist, psychiatrist and physician knows very well that man is imperfect. It stands to reason that if we were perfect, then those above professions, whose occupation it is to "fix" man's imperfection, would be jobless.

Sin is the cause of man's imperfection, and the only lasting remedy is found in forgiveness through the substitutionary sacrifice of Jesus Christ.

 ## Why did God allow sin into the world?

 Although this question originates with a deep-seated rebellion against the Creator, it is often asked; therefore, it deserves an answer. The Bible explains that God is love and love can only be given and received on a free will basis. God presented man with a choice right from the beginning: "...Of every tree of the garden thou mayest freely eat: But of the tree of the knowledge of good and evil, thou shalt not eat of it: for in the day that thou eatest thereof thou shalt surely die" (Genesis 2:16–17). At that point in time, man was perfect, sinless, and had complete fellowship with his Creator. But all of that changed when the deceiver, who manifested himself in the form of a serpent, entered the picture and challenged God's Word: "Yea, hath God said, Ye shall not eat of every tree of the garden?" (Genesis 3:1). This first religious discussion about God's Word ended in a sinful act that carried lasting consequences: "And when the woman saw that the tree was good for food, and that it was pleasant to the eyes, and a tree to be desired to make one wise, she took of the fruit thereof, and did eat, and gave also unto her husband with her; and he did eat" (Genesis 3:6). Man has been separated from fellowship with the living God since that day. Man made a conscious decision to disobey God and fell prey to Satan's temptation.

 If man started out sinless, then how did sin originate?

 Isaiah 14:12–14 says: "How art thou fallen from heaven, O Lucifer, son of the morning! how art thou cut down to the ground, which didst weaken the nations! For thou has said in thine heart, I will ascend into heaven, I will exalt my throne above the stars of God: I

will sit also upon the mount of the congregation, in the sides of the north: I will ascend above the heights of the clouds; I will be like the most High." The prideful "I will" attitude gave birth to sin. Ezekiel describes the anointed cherub's former glory in chapter 28:13–15: "Thou hast been in Eden the garden of God; every precious stone was thy covering, the sardius, topaz, and the diamond, the beryl, the onyx, and the jasper, the sapphire, the emerald, and the carbuncle, and gold: the workmanship of thy tabrets and of thy pipes was prepared in thee in the day that thou wast created. Thou art the anointed cherub that covereth; and I have set thee so: thou wast upon the holy mountain of God; thou hast walked up and down in the midst of the stones of fire. Thou wast perfect in thy ways from the day that thou wast created, till iniquity was found in thee." Satan, the anointed cherub, was not deceived, but sin was born with him. Thus, he is outside the realm of salvation.

Verse 12 provides further clarification: "Son of man, take up a lamentation upon the king of Tyrus, and say unto him, Thus saith the Lord GOD; Thou sealest up the sum, full of wisdom, and perfect in beauty" (Ezekiel 28:12). This is addressed to the king of Tyrus. Is Satan the king of Tyrus? No. But the king of Tyrus is an embodiment of pride, arrogance and selfishness, which are all characteristics of the devil. Sin originated with Satan.

How did God intend to redeem man and save him from his sin?

In Genesis 3:9, God asked Adam: "Where art thou?" How did Adam answer? "...I heard thy voice in the garden, and I was afraid, because I was naked..." (verse 10). That's a rather strange response, because verse 7 says: "...and they sewed fig leaves together, and made themselves aprons." They made a covering of fig leaves to hide their nakedness. The fact that Adam admitted he was naked reveals that he recognized the insufficiency of covering his nakedness with the fig leaves. Later, in verse 21, we read: "Unto Adam also and to his wife did the LORD God make coats of skins, and clothed them."

Important to add is that not only was man's fellowship with God broken by sin, but so was the perfect marriage. Verse 20 says: "And Adam called his wife's name Eve...." Genesis 5:2 says that God called both man and woman by one name: "Male and female created he them; and blessed them, and called their name Adam, in the day when they were created."

God confronted Adam and asked: "Hast thou eaten of the tree...?" Adam blamed his wife: "The woman whom thou gavest to be with me." God asked Eve, "What is this that thou hast done?" Adam pointed an accusing finger at Eve, and she passed the blame to the serpent: "The serpent beguiled me and I did eat." God takes every one seriously. He requires an answer from each of us, so He turned to the serpent and said, "...I will put enmity between thee and the woman, and between thy seed and her seed; it shall bruise thy head, and thou shalt bruise his heel" (Genesis 3:15). This was God's first promise of redemption for mankind: "...and her seed; it shall bruise thy head...." In other words, salvation was to come. God had a plan right from the beginning: He would redeem fallen man, thereby restoring perfect fellowship. Thus, in the first pages of the Bible, God makes it clear that the power through which He will redeem mankind will not be by the seed of man, but by the seed of the woman. This is the first indication as to how God intended to redeem mankind, which had fallen hopelessly into sin and had become subject to Satan.

THE PEOPLE
OF SALVATION

 If God was planning to send a Savior into the world, then why did He choose a nation?

 A family was required in order to bring forth the seed of the woman that would bruise Satan's head. But first, God had to find someone who believed in Him unconditionally. That someone was a man named Abraham, who is referred to in the New Testament as the "father of all who believe." Although Abraham had every reason in the world not to believe God, he did so by faith. The Bible says that by faith Abraham believed God; he obeyed and followed His instruction to leave his father's house and enter into a strange land. The Bible says this about Abraham's wife: "Through faith also Sara herself received strength to conceive seed, and was delivered of a child when she was past age, because she judged him faithful who had promised" (Hebrews 11:11).

God revealed His intention regarding salvation through Abraham: "By faith Abraham, when he was tried, offered up Isaac: and he that had received the promises offered up his only begotten son" (Hebrews 11:17). That was a real test of faith. Sarah had finally conceived and they received the son God promised them; the one for whom they had prayed for more than 25 years. They were both well past the age of childbearing, but the unthinkable occurred and Isaac was born. Then God commanded Abraham to go to Mount Moriah and sacrifice Isaac as an offering. This request seemed ludicrous, yet the Bible says that Abraham obeyed God's command. He wasn't afraid that God could and would do the impossible. Verse 19 confirms: "Accounting that God was able to raise him up, even from the dead; from whence also he received him in a figure."

Now a covenant between God and man was established through Abraham, who believed God. From that point God would reveal His intention through the Law, which was delivered some 400 years later—after Moses led the children of Israel out of Egypt's bondage. But Abraham is the beginning of Israel, God's chosen nation. And Israel is the father of the twelve tribes, of which Judah became the chosen one. Hence all the people of Israel became known as Jews. Later, Jesus said, "Salvation is of the Jews."

What was the purpose of the Law if not to bring salvation?

 The purpose of the Law was to reveal sin. For example, if you drove down a highway that had no posted speed limit, you could go as fast as you wanted to go. But if you were driving down a highway with a posted speed limit, you would be found guilty of breaking the law if you exceeded that limit. God brought up His people, teaching them to obey His commands expressed in His laws. This was necessary so that God would have contact with man through faith. If man believed God and obeyed His law, then a contact was established: faith through obedience. Subsequently, God could give more instructions and details about His intention for His people and fallen mankind.

 ## Does God still consider Israel His chosen people?

 Absolutely! It is very important to remember that God's covenant with the Jews is based solely on His expressed will and faithfulness. Historically, Israel repeatedly has broken God's law; they have been disobedient and rebellious. Nevertheless, God used Jeremiah the prophet to write the following words regarding His people: "Thus saith the LORD; If my covenant be not with day and night, and if I have not appointed the ordinances of heaven and earth...If those ordinances depart from before me, saith the LORD, then the seed of Israel also shall cease from being a nation before me for ever" (Jeremiah 33:25; 31:36). The message is clear: As long as the sun continues to rise, and the moon and stars are still visible at night, Israel will continue to be a nation before God.

This is important because Israel was not a nation and the Jews were scattered all over the world for 2,000 years. However, from God's perspective, it was only a minor intermission in His eternal plan of salvation; Israel never ceased to exist as a nation.

 Are all who are Jews by birth considered God's chosen people?

God's chosen people are the descendants of Abraham, Isaac and Jacob. The first time we find the word "Jews" in Scripture is in 2nd Kings 16:6. Two kingdoms existed during that time: Israel and Judah. Later, the kingdom of Israel was dissolved: "Therefore the LORD was very angry with Israel, and removed them out of his sight: there was none left but the tribe of Judah only" (2nd Kings 17:18). No additional promises were given to the ten-tribe kingdom of Israel, which had separated itself from the tribe of Judah. Judah, however, continues to be Israel. When we read "...was none left but the tribe of Judah only," it includes the tribes of Benjamin and Levi.

What is the difference between Judah and Israel?

 The Bible documents that a remnant of all the tribes of Israel joined themselves to the tribe of Judah: "...out of all the tribes of Israel such as set their hearts to seek the LORD God of Israel came to Jerusalem, to sacrifice unto the LORD God of their fathers" (2nd Chronicles 11:16). Then, in chapter 15:9, we read, "And he gathered all Judah and Benjamin, and the strangers with them out of Ephraim and Manasseh, and out of Simeon: for they fell to him out of Israel in abundance, when they saw that the LORD his God was with him." Thus, we see that the remnant of the ten tribes was added to the tribe of Judah, and in Judah the remnant retained its identity.

After the ten-tribe Israel was defeated, the kingdom destroyed and the people deported, they ceased to exist as a national identity. This corresponds to the prophecy that Jacob, the first Israelite, made: "The sceptre shall not depart from Judah, nor a lawgiver from between his feet, until Shiloh come; and unto him shall the gathering of the people be" (Genesis 49:10).

Long after the ten-tribe Israel had disappeared, God spoke through Ezekiel addressing "the house of Israel" several times in chapter 3, but this "house of Israel" consisted only of Jews; that means all 12 tribes.

Later, when the Church was founded and the Temple still stood in Jerusalem, the Apostle Peter addressed the Jews in Jerusalem as, "Ye men of Israel" (Acts 2:22). In summary, all Jews are Israelites, but not all Israelites are Jews.

 ### Despite their outward religiosity, why is Israel a predominantly secular nation?

 The Bible says that Israel's return will take place while they remain in their unbelief. The change of the people of Israel is described in Ezekiel 36:26: "A new heart also will I give you, and a new spirit will I put within you: and I will take away the stony heart out of your flesh, and I will give you an heart of flesh." Notice that this is a "new" spirit, not "His" spirit. The Jews who return to Israel will experience a change, but not a conversion. They aren't coming back because of their belief in God, but because of existence, security and identity. Since 1948, they have built a political, military and economic identity to be reckoned with. But that's only the beginning. Verse 27 continues: "And I will put my spirit within you, and cause you to walk in my statutes, and ye shall keep my judgments, and do them." That is Israel's future, their national conversion. It will happen after the Church from among the Gentiles has been completed. Paul explains, "For I would not, brethren, that ye should be ignorant of this mystery, lest ye should be wise in your own conceits; that blindness in part is happened to Israel, until the fulness of the Gentiles be come in. And so all Israel shall be saved: as it is written, There shall come out of Sion the Deliverer, and shall turn away ungodliness from Jacob" (Romans 11:25–26).

What we are seeing now is the beginning of the fulfillment of Ezekiel 39:28: "Then shall they know that I am the LORD their God, which caused them to be led into captivity among the heathen: but I have gathered them unto their own land, and have left none of them any more there." Not a single Jew will be left in any other country; they will all return to Israel.

Who owns the land of Israel today?

The answer to this question is fiercely debated between the Jews and Arabs who live in Israel and their surrounding neighbor states. It seems as though the entire world gets involved when it comes to the ownership of the land of Israel. It is rather significant that not a single country sides with the territorial boundaries God ordained and preserved in His Word. The deed to the land of Israel clearly states that the Jews are the original and only legitimate owners defined by geographical references. Genesis 15:18 says: "In the same day the LORD made a covenant with Abram, saying, Unto thy seed have I given this land, from the river of Egypt unto the great river, the river Euphrates." Notice that this resolution is written in the past tense, "...have I given this land...."

Of course, the world disregards what the Bible says about this land and its people, so let's look at it from a political perspective. Israel fought five major wars against its Arab neighbors and was victorious each time. But something strange happened; Israel was not allowed to keep the territory it had conquered. Why not? The nations of the world, particularly the United States, have pressured Israel into surrendering areas of the Promised Land to the Arabs, from whom the Jews conquered the land. This is unusual because every country was established by the force of weapons. For example, Germany lost the war against communism and the rest of the world. As a result, its victors took possession of almost one-third of the country. East Prussia, the part of Germany in which I was born, and where my family's roots date back over 800 years, was divided into Lithuania, Russia and Poland. Why? Because Germany lost the war.

Our own country was established on the basis of force. The Indians lost the battle against the Americans, which settled the land conflict.

All other nations have been able to enjoy the spoils of their victory, but Israel has been denied this right. All of the nations that have conquered territory by force to establish their borders now condemn Israel for taking possession of their own territory. From such a perspective, we can understand God's wrath upon the nations as documented in Joel 3:2, which ends with three accusatory words to the nations: parted my land.

 Why does the world oppose Israel's possession of the Promised Land?

 Because the world lies in darkness. Satan, the god of this world, has blinded the eyes of the people so that they simply cannot see the truth.

Another reason is that all the world will have to condemn themselves before the Judgment Seat of God when they must account for what they have done either for or against His people. Virtually every country has been established by force and violence, yet all the nations' borders are accepted in accordance with their success in using violence to establish their boundaries. They call it international legal borders recognized by the United Nations. The world makes an exception where Israel is concerned; not only do they consider the borders established by God Himself invalid, but they ignore the fact that Israel has also legitimately secured these borders through the action of war.

How did the statement, "His blood be on us, and our children" affect the Jews?

 The suffering of the Jewish people throughout history is the fulfillment of Bible prophecy. Deuteronomy 28:1–14 lists the blessings Israel would experience if they followed the laws of the Lord. But in the next 54 verses, Moses, a servant of God, prophesied what would happen if Israel failed to heed the Word of God.

While the Jews accepted the guilt for the shedding of Jesus' blood, the Apostle Peter makes it quite clear that the entire world was involved, "...both Herod, and Pontius Pilate, with the Gentiles, and the people of Israel..." (Acts 4:27). We are ALL guilty of the shedding of Jesus' blood. But the good news is that ALL people can be saved because of His shed blood!

Professor David Flüsser, New Testament teacher at Jerusalem's Hebrew University, did not believe in Jesus, but during one of our conferences, he said, "If the blood of Jesus is the saving substance for the Christian, would this same blood not have the saving power for the Jews when they said, 'His blood be upon us and our children'"?

Whom do the Jews believe that Isaiah is referring to in chapter 53?

 Isaiah 53 very clearly describes the Messiah who paid the ultimate price for the sins of Israel and the world. This is a difficult chapter for the Jews who do not believe that Jesus is the Messiah. They try to identify the suffering servant as the Jews. While on one hand this could be understood because the Jews have suffered more than any other group of people, this Scripture is not referring to a group of people; it's referring to an individual, a man named Jesus Christ.

It is impossible to deny that this passage is describing Jesus. Verse 7 says, "...he is brought as a lamb to the slaughter, and as a sheep before her shearers is dumb, so he openeth not his mouth." He was crucified between two robbers. Verse 9 says, "...he made his grave with the wicked..." and was buried in a rich man's tomb, "...and with the rich in his death...." Peter wrote, "Who did no sin, neither was guile found in his mouth" (1st Peter 2:22). Isaiah testified, "Neither any deceit in his mouth" and the last verse again mentions the two criminals he was crucified between: "...he was numbered with the transgressors; and he bare the sin of many, and made intercession for the transgressors." This chapter contains too many details that describe a person, a man, that cannot apply to a nation or group of people.

How will the statement, "...they shall look upon Him whom they have pierced," be fulfilled when those who were alive at Jesus' crucifixion are long gone?

This refers to the identity of a people: Israel. Until this day, the Jewish people blatantly reject the truth that Jesus is the Messiah. Romans 11:28 says, "As concerning the gospel, they are enemies for your sakes: but as touching the election, they are beloved for the fathers' sakes." So as a people—to be precise, God's chosen people—they pierced Him and still reject Him until this very day, although the actual piercing was done by a Roman soldier. Here we see demonstrated a national, collective guilt. A more modern example would be to say that the Germans killed the Jews; however, virtually no one who actually did the killing is alive today, yet the guilt is still there and the Germans will have to deal with that guilt for many years to come.

Will the Jews ever possess the land of Israel according to the borders documented in the Bible?

 God's promises to Israel are unconditional; therefore, the Jews will take possession of the land from the Euphrates River to the River of Egypt in due time: "In the same day the LORD made a covenant with Abram, saying, Unto thy seed have I given this land, from the river of Egypt unto the great river, the river Euphrates" (Genesis 15:18). According to this verse, portions of today's Lebanon, Syria, Jordan and Egypt are literally Arab-occupied Israeli territory.

 ## How will the Jews be saved?

 The Jews will be saved by the appearance of the Messiah and on the basis of His shed blood. When Jesus returns, and His feet stand upon the Mount of Olives, the Jews will look upon Him whom they had pierced. God will do something special at that moment: "And I will pour upon the house of David, and upon the inhabitants of Jerusalem, the spirit of grace and of supplications: and they shall look upon me whom they have pierced, and they shall mourn for him, as one mourneth for his only son, and shall be in bitterness for him, as one that is in bitterness for his firstborn" (Zechariah 12:10). The Jews will be saved as an act of God's grace — the same grace that saved each one of us. The cause of their salvation is Jesus, the Son of God, the Messiah of Israel and the Savior of the world. What happened to us will happen to them: "Blotting out the handwriting of ordinances that was against us, which was contrary to us, and took it out of the way, nailing it to his cross" (Colossians 2:14).

CHAPTER
3

JERUSALEM AND THE TEMPLE

 Will Jerusalem be redivided in the future?

 From Israel's perspective, Jerusalem was officially recognized as a free city in 1967, during the Six-Day War, and was declared as Israel's indivisible capital city for eternity. Obviously, recent developments show that the nations do not agree with that declaration. No nation stands behind the Jewish people or their claim to all of Jerusalem.

During the 19-year Jordanian occupation of Jerusalem, the city was divided by a wall, barricades and barbed wire. All of these markers were torn down after Jerusalem was liberated. Today, there is barely a trace of the divided city as it once was. Nevertheless, the division on the political scene clearly exists. For example, the United States established a Consulate in both the east and west sections of Jerusalem. Our embassy is not located in Jerusalem, but in Tel Aviv. We emphasize the United States in particular because America is still considered to be Israel's "best friend"; so if this "friend" is actually an enemy, it makes one wonder how bad Israel's enemies are.

 ## Who owns the Temple Mount?

Israeli territory includes all of Jerusalem, and that means the Temple Mount. However, it's not as simple as it sounds, or as it should be. The Arabs— the ones living not only in Israel but in all of the Arab countries—vehemently oppose Israel's sovereignty over the Temple Mount.

Viewing the religious side of the spectrum, Muslim authorities have made it clear that the Temple Mount, Jerusalem, and all of Israel belong to the Arabs. Muslim law dictates that wherever and whenever territory is con-quered in the name of Allah, it becomes the eternal prop-erty of the Muslims.

However, God has different ideas, which He expressed through the Jewish prophet Zechariah, who wrote: "So the angel that communed with me said unto me, Cry thou, saying, Thus saith the LORD of hosts; I am jealous for Jerusalem and for Zion with a great jealousy. And I am very sore displeased with the heathen that are at ease: for I was but a little displeased, and they helped forward the affliction. Therefore thus saith the LORD; I am returned to Jerusalem with mercies: my house shall be built in it, saith the LORD of hosts, and a line shall be stretched forth upon Jerusalem" (Zechariah 1:14–16). The ques-tion of ownership will be settled once and for all when the Messiah returns.

 ## When will the Temple be built in Jerusalem?

 There is no doubt that the Temple will be built in Jerusalem. The prophets clearly state that the Temple must be rebuilt and sacrifices reinstituted so that the Antichrist can order them to cease during the Great Tribulation. Logically, if there is no Temple, there will be no sacrifices; if there are no sacrifices, there will be no need for the Antichrist to order them to cease.

Jesus referred to the Temple in Matthew 24 when He quoted the prophet Daniel: "When ye therefore shall see the abomination of desolation, spoken of by Daniel the prophet, stand in the holy place, (whoso readeth, let him understand:)" (verse 15). And Daniel makes this point very clear when he wrote: "And he shall confirm the covenant with many for one week: and in the midst of the week he shall cause the sacrifice and the oblation to cease..." (Daniel 9:27). This is clearly the future.

The Temple will be built during the Great Tribulation. The Antichrist will set himself up in the Temple and will declare himself to be God. Of course, this also applies to the spiritual temple in which the Antichrist will have taken up residence. There are millions of "believers" who have no idea who the Jesus of the Bible actually is, and who blindly follow the dictates of a false Jesus. Obviously, the Jews cannot stand "in the holy place" if none exists. Although the Temple must be rebuilt, it is virtually impossible to speculate when that will take place.

How many times has the Temple been built and destroyed?

The first Temple was destroyed by Babylon, the first Gentile superpower, under the leadership of King Nebuchadnezzar. The second Temple was rebuilt under the leadership of King Cyrus of Persia, the second Gentile superpower. That Temple was destroyed in 70 A.D. by Rome, the fourth and final Gentile superpower.

Can the Jews reinstitute Temple service without the Ark of the Covenant?

The Jews can literally do anything they want because during the time of the Antichrist's rule, they will become so deceived that any and all compromises will be possible. Therefore, the Temple can be rebuilt and sacrificial services reinstituted without the Ark of the Covenant or the ashes of the red heifer. At this point, the majority of Jewish people are ready to do just about anything for the sake of peace, and when that moment comes, they will be all too happy to follow the deceptive dictates of the Antichrist. But illusion will end in a rude awakening in the midst of the Tribulation when the Antichrist sits in the Temple and declares that he is God.

 ## Where is the Ark of the Covenant?

The Ark of the Covenant is not mentioned in Scripture after the Jews returned from Babylonian captivity. It stands to reason that it was probably seized and eventually destroyed. There have been many reports about the discovery of the Ark, and each one has been exposed as a hoax. These fables have only served as a platform to place the authors of such presumptuous claims in the spotlight. The Ark of the Covenant has never been found and, according to Jeremiah 3:16, it never will because it no longer exists: "And it shall come to pass, when ye be multiplied and increased in the land, in those days, saith the LORD, they shall say no more, The ark of the covenant of the LORD: neither shall it come to mind: neither shall they remember it; neither shall they visit it; neither shall that be done any more."

48

If the Temple sacrifices only acted as a sin "covering," and Jesus' blood is the power for the remission of sins, then why would Temple sacrifices need to be reinstituted?

The Holy Spirit inspired Hosea to write a significant prophecy: "For the children of Israel shall abide many days without a king, and without a prince, and without a sacrifice, and without an image, and without an ephod, and without teraphim" (Hosea 3:4). This indicates an undefined period of time when the Jews will not have these things that belong to their cultural and religious identity, including the Temple service. It is my understanding that the rebuilding of the Temple, with the reinstitution of the sacrificial service, will be done as a memorial to what Jesus accomplished on Calvary's cross. The Jews never really fully understood what the Temple service was all about, but when Jesus comes they will understand why it was necessary for countless animals to be sacrificed. Then the Jews will serve the Lord with joy and gladness.

Why is it necessary for the Temple to exist during the Millennium, described in Ezekiel 40–48?

 The Temple description in Ezekiel 40–48 is not identical to the previous Temples that stood upon Mount Moriah. But this Temple will be erected and sacrifices will take place. Why? Because it is a memorial to the salvation that took place through Jesus Christ. In the same manner with which we take communion as a remembrance of the death of our Lord, which took place almost 2,000 years ago, yet He lives forevermore, so, too, will the Temple service be operated.

 Are any preparations to rebuild the Temple taking place now?

 Yes. Two Jerusalem-based institutions are concerning themselves with the rebuilding of the Temple. The first group is known as "The Temple Mount Faithful," whose members have sworn never to surrender the sovereignty of Mount Moriah to anyone outside of the Jewish people. The second group is "The Temple Institute." Their task is to duplicate the utensils and priestly garments required for the Temple ceremony. However, these two groups, in addition to various splinter groups, are not officially recognized by the Jewish religious authority. They do not represent Judaism. I have been told that the largest following of these organizations is a group evangelical Christians who are fascinated by the success of manufacturing utensils for the new Temple. Nevertheless, these two institutions show that Israel's desire to have the Temple on Mount Moriah must not be taken lightly. We must remember that Israel is located in the center of the world, Jerusalem is the center of Israel, and the Temple is the center of Jerusalem. Contained in the Temple was the Holy of Holies and the Ark of the Covenant, where the two tablets on which the Law of God was written. In other words, the center of Israel for worldwide Judaism is still missing.

 Is it possible for the new Temple to be built in our days? .

 This theory has been debated, and in some instances, has been accepted by a number of respected scholars and theologians. However, at this point it is impossible, because the Muslims stand in violent opposition to anything that might benefit the Jews. Nevertheless, nothing is impossible when it comes to politics, even religious politics. Things can change overnight, as we witnessed with the fall of communism. Without any warning or prediction, communism imploded and the world watched in jubilation as the Berlin Wall, a symbol of communism, was knocked down by the people who built it.

If the new Temple will be used by the Antichrist, can't it be built in our days?

It sounds reasonable, but that is only speculation. We know that the Antichrist will come with cleverness and deception. He will be a master politician, a great negotiator, and one who will perform miracles in the sight of all men. Such a character could very well be capable of negotiating a peace treaty between the Arabs and Jews in Israel. As a result, it is not unthinkable that a Temple will be built beside the Dome of the Rock on

Mount Moriah, demonstrating peace to the world. That Jews and Muslims could pray on the Temple Mount in unity was previously unthinkable. But this Temple will indeed be used by the Antichrist, because the Bible says, "Who opposeth and exalteth himself above all that is called God, or that is worshipped; so that he as God sitteth in the temple of God, shewing himself that he is God" (2nd Thessalonians 2:4).

 ## Is Jerusalem Jewish or international?

 Consider these words: "...and Jerusalem shall be trodden down of the Gentiles, until the times of the Gentiles be fulfilled" (Luke 21:24). At this time, the Gentiles still have charge over Israel, particularly Jerusalem. Two powerful religious elements play a decisive role in Jerusalem's immediate future: the Arab Muslims and the Roman Catholic Vatican. Both powers vehemently oppose Jewish sovereignty over Jerusalem. We must also remember that the city will be divided into three parts: "And the great city was divided into three parts..." (Revelation 16:19).

The Vatican, the United Nations and the European Union agree that Jerusalem should be an international city. In other words, they believe it should be controlled by the United Nations or some other international body. For all practical purposes, it is not a united city today and it will become international because of Gentile force. Revelation 11:8 says: "...the great city, which spiritually is called Sodom and Egypt...." Which city is that? The verse continues: "...where also our Lord was crucified." That's Jerusalem. The ultimate liberation will come when Jesus returns and stands upon the Mount of Olives, which is east of Jerusalem.

Will peace come to Israel?

Yes. The Jews will experience peace. But they will experience two types: temporary and eternal. At the time of this writing, it is all but impossible for the Jews and Arabs to negotiate a mutual peace, but that doesn't mean that it is impossible. Political developments can change overnight. If the right man says the right thing at the right time, a peace treaty can very well be implemented. But the agreement must be more than a piece of paper; it must be a treaty in which both the Arabs and Jews actually believe. This must come about because the Bible says that they shall say "peace and safety." In other words, there will be peace; otherwise, they would not be able to say "peace and safety."

THE CHURCH

 There are literally thousands of denominations; how can we identify the true Church?

 The true Church is where the presence of Christ dwells. Jesus said: "...where two or three are gathered together in my name, there am I in the midst of them" (Matthew 18:20). Thus the next question is: Which Christ? The real Christ is He who identified Himself through the prophets. Isaiah wrote, "He was oppressed, and he was afflicted, yet he opened not his mouth: he is brought as a lamb to the slaughter, and as a sheep before her shearers is dumb, so he openeth not his mouth" (Isaiah 53:7). That's the real Jesus! The Lamb of God who was brought to the slaughter, who did not open His mouth in protest. When we follow Him, we find ourselves on the narrow path that leads to eternal glory.

 ## How can I recognize the true Church?

The Church can be found wherever two or three born-again believers gather together in His name. The Church isn't an organization or institution. It is not represented by any denomination or local charter. The Church is an organism that has been grafted into the olive tree, which is Israel. Therefore, any church, regardless of its name or denomination, can contain the true Church, consisting of born-again believers. This is the Church that Jesus identified and promised to build. We should never be misled into thinking that our organizational structure, denomination, local church, missionary organization, or any other "religious" entity represents the true Church of Jesus Christ on earth. Any Christian institution in its function and office may only serve as a scaffold for the building of the Church. Let me explain: During times of construction, we see a seemingly confusing amount of tools, building material, dirt, sand, machinery, and cranes. The scaffold is the structure that usually surrounds the building while it's under construction. When the building is finished, the scaffold and all the other equipment is removed and then the beautiful new building is revealed.

In a spiritual sense, we are a building of which the Apostle Peter wrote, "Ye also, as lively stones, are built up a spiritual house, an holy priesthood, to offer up spiritual sacrifices, acceptable to God by Jesus Christ" (1st Peter 2:5). These "lively stones" are the born-again believers. But nothing from this "spiritual house" is visible. The Church of Jesus Christ would not be destroyed even if every church and Christian institution closed this very day.

 ## Will Jesus bring peace?

 Of course He will. He is peace in person. He gives us the peace that passes all understanding. But there is another side of Jesus that He revealed in His own words: "Think not that I am come to send peace on earth: I came not to send peace, but a sword. For I am come to set a man at variance against his father, and the daughter against her mother, and the daughter-in-law against her mother-in-law. And a man's foes shall be they of his own household" (Matthew 10:34–36). Notice that Jesus said "a sword," not peace, in this passage of Scripture. It is the two-edged sword of the Word of God that even divides families. Those who allow themselves to be judged by the Word will enter into the peace that is eternal.

Why is this false gospel so successful?

This false gospel is so successful because it pleases man, builds self and seeks to elevate sinful man to God's level. The false gospel is built on man's natural desire to "do" something toward gaining salvation.

Furthermore, the success of the false gospel is also based on the visible. This is particularly true with the prosperity "gospel," which teaches that you will become wealthy if you follow certain steps. Such teaching appeals to man's ego because we like to be successful, healthy and wealthy. If there is a way to obtain such a position, we will gladly dedicate our lives towards that goal. This is not only the case with the false gospel, but it applies to virtually all other religions.

But true Christianity differs from all other religions. We confess that we are hopelessly lost without Jesus; we recognize that we are sinful by nature, and we confirm and confess that there is not one who is righteous among us. We depend on God's grace. We understand that it is impossible for us to attain the holiness and righteousness God requires. We need the One who has paid the ultimate price to atone for the irreparable damage we have caused through sin. That price was the blood Jesus shed on Calvary's cross. He did not repair us, but renewed us by the power of the Holy Spirit. It is our duty to stress this warning to those who emphasize only one side of the Gospel—peace, joy, love, prosperity, health and happiness—without telling the other side, which includes trial, tribulation, suffering and persecution.

 ### Will Christians experience persecution?

 Persecution is a part of the Church's existence. Believers have been persecuted right from the start in Jerusalem, then later by the Roman institution. Many members of the Church continue to suffer until this very day. Historically, the Church has also suffered persecution under communism, at the hand of Muslims and other religions. Every child of God will experience a certain measure of tribulation. Sometimes tribulations can manifest themselves physically, and other times they can attack our spiritual lives to the point that we doubt our salvation. But that does not mean that we should expect open persecution in all parts of the world. This contradicts the verses that admonish us to obey our government and to try to live at peace with all men. Furthermore, deception does not run parallel to persecution. You can't deceive someone by persecuting him.

 ## How can we recognize deception?

Knowing your Bible is the best defense against falling prey to deception. When you hear one-sided Gospel messages, such as those that proclaim "Jesus will make you happy, healthy and wealthy," you are sitting under dangerous teaching. Jesus was despised and rejected. He prophesied that the Church is a small flock.

Paul confirmed that the Church's calling is mostly from among the rejected: "For ye see your calling, brethren, how that not many wise men after the flesh, not many mighty, not many noble, are called: But God hath chosen the foolish things of the world to confound the wise; and God hath chosen the weak things of the world to confound the things which are mighty" (1st Corinthians 1:26–27). If you are grounded in the truth of God's Word, then you should be able to immediately recognize deception as soon as you hear a one-sided Jesus being taught. We do not deny that Jesus offers an abundant life and can certainly grant you happiness, health and wealth, but that may be the exception because, as we have just seen, the Bible portrays the Church in a much different light.

 ## What is "another" gospel?

"Another" gospel can be defined as one that targets self-gratification. It is a "gospel" that offers another Jesus who can benefit you in the flesh by denying the cross. To the church at Philippi, Paul wrote, "(For many walk, of whom I have told you often, and now tell you even weeping, that they are the enemies of the cross of Christ..." (Philippians 3:18).

What is the future of the Church?

Eternity! The Church is destined to be in the presence of the Lord, who is its Head. Therefore, regardless of any development, no matter how negative, that may occur during our days, the Church is eternal. We are His Body, and we are also His Bride, who eagerly awaits the coming of the Bridegroom.

What is the difference between the Body of Christ and the Bride of Christ?

According to Ephesians 1:10–23, the Church is referred to as Jesus' Body, while Ephesians 5:25–27 and Revelation 19:7 refer to her also as the Bride. How can the Church be the Bride and His Body at the same time? Eve was taken from Adam's body, yet she was also his bride. This is also expressed with the words, "Husbands love your wives, even as Christ also loved the church."

Are there two Second Comings?

Yes, the Lord will return in two phases: First, He will come in the clouds of heaven (not on earth) to collect His Bride, which is the Church. Then He will come with His saints, seven years after the Rapture, and His feet will stand upon the Mount of Olives.

Understanding the two phases of His Second Coming is critical. In 2nd Thessalonians chapter 2:2–3, the Apostle Paul warned, "...That ye be not soon shaken in mind, or be troubled, neither by spirit, nor by word, nor by letter as from us, as that the day of Christ is at hand. Let no man deceive you by any means: for that day shall not come, except there come a falling away first, and that man of sin be revealed, the son of perdition." When we read this passage of Scripture, it seems to be saying that the Rapture cannot occur before the Antichrist is revealed. However, such is not the case. Paul is speaking of two events: 1) the coming of our Lord Jesus and 2) our gathering together unto Him. The day of Christ is not the Rapture, but it is His coming in great power and glory.

The Apostle had already written to the Thessalonians and described the Rapture in his first letter. So obviously with the confusion that was caused, Paul disappointedly asked, "Remember ye not, that, when I was yet with you, I told you these things?" (verse 5). Apparently they had forgotten that the removal of the light must take place before the Day of Christ can take place. In 2nd Thessalonians 2:6, Paul revealed this fact with the words, "And now ye know what withholdeth that he might be revealed in his time." The Church, the light of this world, is the element that is hindering the power of darkness.

Another reason that Jesus cannot physically come back to earth before the Church has been removed is the role of the Comforter. Jesus said, "...It is expedient for you that I go away: for if I go not away, the Comforter will not come unto you; but if I depart, I will send him unto you" (John 16:7). That verse clears things up; Jesus Christ, the suffering servant and the Holy Spirit, in the office of the Comforter, cannot be on earth simultaneously. Therefore, the Comforter must be removed so that Jesus can return.

What's the difference between the Rapture and the Second Coming?

A number of verses in Scripture define these two

important events, but the main ingredient is the Lord Himself. For instance, the Lord does not come to earth when the Church is raptured. The Bible says that we will meet Him in the clouds of heaven. The Second Coming is defined by the prophecy that says, "And his feet shall stand on the mount of Olives." The Second Coming is the fulfillment of His ascension from the Mount of Olives. Acts 1:11 says, "...Ye men of Galilee, why stand ye gazing up into heaven? this same Jesus, which is taken up from you into heaven, shall so come in like manner as ye have seen him go into heaven." Many references for the Second Coming are scattered throughout the Old and New Testament. On the other hand, no signs precede the Rapture of the Church, with the exception of the repetitious admonition to always be ready: "Looking for that blessed hope, and the glorious appearing of the great God and our Saviour Jesus Christ...So Christ was once offered to bear the sins of many; and unto them that look for him shall he appear the second time without sin unto salvation" (Titus 2:13; Hebrews 9:28).

When will the Rapture take place?

The Rapture will take place when the last from among the Gentiles has been saved. This not only will, but must happen before the beginning of the Great Tribulation. Why? Because the Great Tribulation is the result of the Church's removal. The Great Tribulation cannot begin unless and until the Holy Spirit, who indwells the believer, has been removed.

A number of examples of this can be found in the Old Testament. Let's take a closer look at one. During Lot's time, the angels announced to him that Sodom and Gomorrah would be destroyed. Lot was urged to run for his life. During that episode, something significant was revealed; the hindering element for Sodom and Gomorrah's judgment was righteous Lot. The Bible says, "I cannot do anything until thou hast been removed hither." God could only implement judgment after the righteous one was removed. This corresponds with Scripture's statement that we, the Church, are not appointed to wrath.

But doesn't the Bible also say that we must enter the kingdom of God through much tribulation? That is true; however, the result of such tribulation is never condemnation but salvation. Peter wrote: "Wherein ye greatly rejoice, though now for a season, if need be, ye are in heaviness through manifold temptations: That the trial of your faith, being much more precious than of gold that perisheth, though it be tried with fire, might be found unto praise and honour and glory at the appearing of Jesus Christ"(1st Peter 1:6–7).

 Can you biblically support your stand on the Pre-Trib Rapture?

"For our conversation is in heaven; from whence also we look for the Saviour, the Lord Jesus Christ" (Philippians 3:20).

"...waiting for the coming of our Lord Jesus Christ" (1st Corinthians 1:7b).

"...ye turned to God from idols to serve the living and true God; And to wait for his Son from heaven, whom he raised from the dead, even Jesus, which delivered us from the wrath to come" (1st Thessalonians 1:9b–10).

"Looking for that blessed hope, and the glorious appearing of the great God and our Saviour Jesus Christ"

(Titus 2:13).

"So Christ was once offered to bear the sins of many; and unto them that look for him shall he appear the second time without sin unto salvation" (Hebrews 9:28).

"...ye yourselves like unto men that wait for their lord..." (Luke 12:36).

The word "wait" implies waiting for Jesus. Scripture does not instruct us to wait for the Antichrist, the beginning of the Great Tribulation, the time of pre-wrath or the Battle of Armageddon. The Lord plainly said that He would come at a time "...when ye think not." These few words expose the Mid-Trib, Pre-Wrath and Post-Tribulation positions as false teachings in a very simple manner.

 ## What will happen after the Rapture occurs?

 Revelation 12:12 reveals what will occur in heaven and on earth following the Rapture of the Church: "Therefore rejoice, ye heavens, and ye that dwell in them. Woe to the inhabitants of the earth and of the sea! for the devil is come down unto you, having great wrath, because he knoweth that he hath but a short

time." In the Old Testament we read repeatedly of the terrible things that will occur on earth. This is also confirmed by the Lord in Matthew 24:21: "For then shall be great tribulation, such as was not since the beginning of the world to this time, no, nor ever shall be." That is why it is called the Great Tribulation, because it has never occurred in such catastrophic proportions as it will during that time. Jesus makes it very clear that this one-time event will never happen again.

DANIEL'S
PROPHECY

Why would the Antichrist take away the daily
sacrifice?

Daniel 8:11 says: "Yea, he magnified himself even
to the prince of the host, and by him the daily sacrifice was taken away, and the place of his sanctuary was
cast down." Furthermore, chapter 9:27 says: "And he
shall confirm the covenant with many for one week: and
in the midst of the week he shall cause the sacrifice and
the oblation to cease, and for the overspreading of abominations he shall make it desolate, even until the consummation, and that determined shall be poured upon the

desolate" (verse 27). His success and self-glory is described in chapter 11:36: "And the king shall do according to his will; and he shall exalt himself, and magnify himself above every god, and shall speak marvellous things against the God of gods, and shall prosper till the indignation be accomplished: for that that is determined shall be done." He calls a stop to the sacrifice because it was ordained by God. He opposes God; therefore, he will have to abolish anything related to God. Furthermore, the Apostle Paul wrote of him in 2nd Thessalonians 2:4: "Who opposeth and exalteth himself above all that is called God, or that is worshipped; so that he as God sitteth in the temple of God, shewing himself that he is God."

 ### How does Nebuchadnezzar's image relate to our days?

 Daniel 2:4 documents the entire Gentile history, including the end, and the setting up of the eternal kingdom which "shall stand for ever."

There are only four Gentile superpowers:

1. Babylon

2. Persia

3. Greece

4. Rome

The prophet occupies himself more with the last power structure (Rome) than any other. Why? Because it's the longest lasting one. Rome controlled the world when Jesus was born and as we will see in the next few chapters, Roman (European) dominance and influence remains global in proportion until this day. But all of the Gentile superpowers, including many others that the Bible does not mention, have no future from an eternal perspective because we read: "And in the days of these kings shall the God of heaven set up a kingdom, which shall never be destroyed: and the kingdom shall not be left to other people, but it shall break in pieces and consume all these kingdoms, and it shall stand for ever. Forasmuch as thou sawest that the stone was cut out of the mountain without hands, and that it brake in pieces the iron, the brass, the clay, the silver, and the gold; the great God hath made known to the king what shall come to pass hereafter: and the dream is certain, and the interpretation thereof sure" (Daniel 2:44–45).

Does the handwriting on the wall in Daniel chapter 5 have any prophetic significance for the endtimes?

Daniel 5 is a great prophetic chapter. Belshazzar represents the nations of the world who live at ease. They are having a party, celebrating their successes. Of particular importance is their religious activity that climaxes with the mixing of the holy with the unholy: "Then they brought the golden vessels that were taken out of the temple of the house of God which was at Jerusalem...They drank wine, and praised the gods of gold, and of silver, of brass, of iron, of wood, and of stone" (Daniel 5:3–4). This should remind us of Revelation 9:20: "...yet repented not of the works of their hands, that they should not worship devils, and idols of gold, and silver, and brass, and stone, and of wood...."

The handwriting on the wall represents Israel. The founding of the state in May 1948 moved the world and continues to grab more headlines than any other country of size.

The event concludes with the infamous interpretation of the words, "Mene, Mene, Tekel, Upharsin" (Daniel 5:25), explained in verse 27: "...Thou art weighed in the balances, and art found wanting." Despite their success in their own right, the nations will be "found wanting."

What are the historical dates of Daniel's 70th week showing that the birth and death of the Messiah has already taken place precisely as prophesied by Daniel?

The 70 weeks correspond with the year 445 B.C., or the twentieth year of Artaxerxes (Nehemiah 2:1–8). Each week represents seven years. I can't explain it any better than Dr. J. Vernon McGee did in his book, *Thru The Bible*, Volume 3, page 588:

> Sixty-two weeks, or 434 years, bring us to the Messiah. Sir Robert Anderson in his book, *The Coming Prince,* has worked out the time schedule. From the first of the month Nisan to the tenth of Nisan (April 6) A.D. 32, are 173,880 days. Dividing them according to the Jewish year of 360 days, he

arrives at 483 years (69 sevens). On this day Jesus rode into Jerusalem, offering Himself for the first time, publicly and officially, as the Messiah.

After the 69 weeks, or 483 years, there is a time break. Between the sixty-ninth and seventieth week two events of utmost importance are to take place:

1. Messiah will be cut off. This was the crucifixion of Christ, the great mystery and truth of the Gospel.

2. Destruction of Jerusalem, which took place in A.D. 70, when Titus the Roman was the instrument.

Daniel wrote, "And after threescore and two weeks shall Messiah be cut off but not for himself." The Hebrew Bible makes this point even clearer: "And after those 62 weeks, the anointed one will disappear and vanish." We entered the endtimes at that point. However, the 70th week has not yet been fulfilled: "And he shall confirm the covenant with many for one week." That's the work of the Antichrist, who will complete the 70th week of years with the Great Tribulation.

What book was Daniel instructed to seal?

Daniel 12:4 says, "But thou, O Daniel, shut up the words, and seal the book, even to the time of the end: many shall run to and fro, and knowledge shall be increased" (verse 4). Verse 9 says: "And he said, Go thy way, Daniel: for the words are closed up and sealed till the time of the end." The words that were closed, or the book that was sealed, was the New Covenant. Daniel confessed that he did not understand: "...how long shall it be to the end of these wonders?...Oh, Lord, what shall be the end of these things?..." Daniel didn't understand, nor did anyone else, until the endtimes. When did the endtimes begin? When Jesus fulfilled His task, dying on Calvary's cross and, at that moment, the veil in the Temple was torn from top to bottom.

Part of the answer is found in Galatians 3:23: "But before faith came, we were kept under the law, shut up unto the faith which should afterwards be revealed." Also, verse 5 says: "He therefore that ministereth to you the Spirit, and worketh miracles among you, doeth he it by the works of the law, or by the hearing of faith?"

When the Church was born on Pentecost, the Apostle

Peter said: "But this is that which was spoken by the prophet Joel; And it shall come to pass in the last days, saith God, I will pour out of my Spirit upon all flesh: and your sons and your daughters shall prophesy, and your young men shall see visions, and your old men shall dream dreams" (Acts 2:16–17).

CHAPTER 6

THE ANTICHRIST

 Who is the Antichrist?

 The Antichrist is Satan's masterpiece. He is a near-perfect imitation of Jesus Christ. He is the world ruler referred to in Scripture as the "son of perdition" (John 17:12; 2nd Thessalonians 2:3); "the lawless one" (2nd Thessalonians 2:8); the "king of fierce countenance" (Daniel 3:23); and a brilliant negotiator who will bring peace to the world.

Daniel offers more insight about the Antichrist and his kingdom in chapter 7:23: "Thus he said, The fourth beast shall be the fourth kingdom upon earth, which shall be diverse from all kingdoms, and shall devour the whole earth, and shall tread it down, and break it in pieces." The word "diverse" is repeated several times in this chapter. We notice that the fourth beast is not limited to one place, but "...shall devour the whole earth." How will he do it? "And his power shall be mighty, but not by his own power: and he shall destroy wonderfully, and shall prosper, and practise, and shall destroy the mighty and the holy people. And through his policy also he shall cause craft to prosper in his hand; and he shall magnify himself in his heart, and by peace shall destroy many: he shall also stand up against the Prince of princes; but he shall be broken without hand" (Daniel 8:24–25).

Notice the words "destroy wonderfully"; "prosper"; "shall cause craft to prosper"; "magnify himself" and "by peace shall destroy many." He is the ultimate leader; he is the success story of the new global world. Notice the words "peaceably," "flatteries" and "deceitfully" in chapter 11:21–24: "And in his estate shall stand up a vile person, to whom they shall not give the honour of the kingdom: but he shall come in peaceably, and obtain the kingdom by flatteries. And with the arms of a flood shall they be overflown from before him, and shall be broken; yea, also the prince of the covenant. And after the league made with him he shall work deceitfully: for he shall come up, and shall become strong with a small people. He shall enter peaceably even upon the fattest places of the province; and he shall do that which his fathers have not done, nor his fathers' fathers; he shall scatter among them the prey, and spoil, and riches: yea, and he shall forecast his devices against the strong holds, even for a time." The word "flatteries" continues to occur in verses 32 and 34. Verse 36 again testifies that he "shall prosper."

The Bible does not identify the Antichrist by name, nor does it tell us that we should search for his identity. But one thing becomes clear: He is the most successful man on earth. The Chinese communists, the Arab Muslims and the world's Churchianity will hail this person as the messiah of the world, the great savior, a miracle worker, and the most benevolent man in history.

Revelation offers additional information: "...and all the world wondered after the beast. And they worshipped the dragon which gave power unto the beast: and they worshipped the beast, saying, Who is like unto the beast?

who is able to make war with him?" (Revelation 13:3–4). Verse 8 says: "And all that dwell upon the earth shall worship him... ." We do well to take careful notice that this man and his system is global, not limited to a certain country or race of people. Finally, the world will have achieved peace and safety, but we know the Bible says that when they say peace and safety, sudden destruction will come upon them.

For those who try to identify the Antichrist, look for a nice guy, a person everybody will love, a politician unlike any other who will promise and fulfill and, as a result, will earn the adoration, even worship, from the world.

 ## Will the Antichrist be a Jew?

 The Antichrist will be a Jew to the Jews and a Gentile to the Gentiles. He will be a man of miracles who can be all things to all people. He will have the ability to bring about peace to mankind so that people will be fooled into thinking they are safe and secure.

He will be a Jew because Jesus prophesied: "...If another shall come in his own name, him ye will receive"

(John 5:43).

Opinions vary on this matter, but I believe that the Antichrist must be a Jew because otherwise, the Jewish people would not accept him as their Messiah.

Daniel revealed an interesting quality about the Antichrist when he wrote, "Neither shall he regard the God of his fathers..." (Daniel 11:37). There is no God other than the God of Abraham, Isaac and Jacob, the God of Israel, the Creator of heaven and earth. The Antichrist will be a renegade Jew who ultimately identifies himself as God.

 ## Why hasn't the Antichrist been revealed yet?

 Second Thessalonians 2:6–7 says: "And now ye know what withholdeth that he might be revealed in his time. For the mystery of iniquity doth already work: only he who now letteth will let, until he be taken out of the way." Darkness cannot overtake the world because the Holy Spirit, which indwells every believer by faith, makes up the light of the world.

Also, the Great Tribulation is God's wrath on earth. To

be more precise, Revelation 6:15–16 says the "wrath of the Lamb." That wrath does not come upon His Bride because Scripture guarantees: "For God hath not appointed us to wrath, but to obtain salvation by our Lord Jesus Christ" (1st Thessalonians 5:9).

The Antichrist is the first beast mentioned in Revelation 13 and the false prophet is the second beast. To whom does the mark belong?

The mark of the beast will belong to all who accept it: "And he causeth all, both small and great, rich and poor, free and bond, to receive a mark in their right hand, or in their foreheads: And that no man might buy or sell, save he that had the mark, or the name of the beast, or the number of his name"(Revelation 13:16–17). But the number of the beast—666— is the number of the Antichrist: "...for it is the number of a man; and his number is Six hundred threescore and six" (Revelation 13:18).

Is there more than one Antichrist?

The Apostle John is the only New Testament writer who actually uses the term "antichrist." Important to note is that in its context, the word "antichrist" should be understood as one who stands in place of Christ as a substitute. His goal is to deceive all people into believing that he is the long-awaited Messiah of the Jews, the great prophet Mohammed for the Muslims, the god-man for the Hindu and Buddhists and the Lord Jesus Christ Himself for Churchianity.

In his first letter, John warned, "Little children, it is the last time: and as ye have heard that antichrist shall come, even now are there many antichrists; whereby we know that it is the last time" (1st John 2:18). These "antichrists" are those people who do a work of deception. But the Antichrist is a person who is possessed by the devil, a fact that is clearly revealed in his end: "And the devil that deceived them was cast into the lake of fire and brimstone, where the beast and the false prophet are, and shall be tormented day and night for ever and ever" (Revelation 20:10).

When will the Antichrist be revealed?

In the previous answer we saw that the spirit of the Antichrist was already at work during the time of the apostles. This spirit is revealed in falsehood — like counterfeit money, it looks real and feels real, but it is not real.

To the church at Corinth, the Apostle Paul cautioned, "For if he that cometh preacheth another Jesus, whom we have not preached, or if ye receive another spirit, which ye have not received, or another gospel, which ye have not accepted, ye might well bear with him" (2nd Corinthians 11:4). This verse clearly refers to "another" Jesus, "another" spirit and "another" gospel. He continues, "For such are false apostles, deceitful workers, transforming themselves into the apostles of Christ" (verse 13). This is important because this verse is not referring to other religions, but to Christendom. This verse is speaking about Jesus, the Spirit, the Gospel, and the apostles. That means that the Antichrist is working his deception among the worldwide work of Christianity. In verse 14, Paul reveals, "...no marvel; for Satan himself is transformed into an angel of light." This is the epitome of deception. Not only does Satan look like an angel of light, but he is actually transformed into an angel of light.

Most of Christianity is unaware that a great deception is taking place within the Church today. It does not matter what denomination the church may be, how fundamental its teachings are, or how serious the Bible is taken; deception means it looks like the real thing, but is, in fact, false. The spirit of the Antichrist is progressively revealed, but the Antichrist in person can and will be revealed only when the Church is removed, because the Church is the light of the world. In contrast, the Antichrist is the epitome of the work of darkness.

 ## How can we recognize the spirit of the Antichrist?

 We must respond with another question: How did Christ look? I am not referring to His physical appearance, because nobody knows. But Scripture contains ample description of how He really was. For example, Isaiah 53:3 says, "He is despised and rejected of men; a man of sorrows, and acquainted with grief: and we hid as it were our faces from him; he was despised, and we esteemed him not."

I think that most readers would agree that Jesus Christ is not preached today to look like one who was despised, rejected or not esteemed. But this scriptural statement gives the first clue as to the real Jesus, the Christ. Therefore, when you hear Jesus being preached in the church, or sung about on the radio, or depicted in literature as the one who offers you a bunch of earthly benefits, that should be the first alarm that a false Jesus is being presented to you.

We do not deny that Jesus can do anything, even the positive things that we so much desire, such as restoring our health, granting us prosperity, renewing our marriages and giving us joy and peace. But that is only one side of the Gospel. Jesus describes the other side of the Gospel in Matthew 24:9–10: "Then shall they deliver you up to be afflicted, and shall kill you: and ye shall be hated of all nations for my name's sake. And then shall many be offended, and shall betray one another, and shall hate one another." The true Gospel message is simple: Those who follow Him will do as He says, will take up their cross and will follow Him (Mark 8:34). Paul defines the Gospel message with these words: "For the preaching of the cross is to them that perish foolishness; but unto us which are saved it is the power of God" (1st Corinthians 1:18).

THE NATIONS

 Which nations play a major endtime role?

Israel will obviously play a major role in endtime events. All of the nations that surround Israel will also be involved, as will Rome, the city/state that ruled Israel when Jesus came to earth the first time. Daniel identified the final Gentile power structure in chapter 9:26: "...after threescore and two weeks shall Messiah be cut off, but not for himself: and the people of the prince that shall come shall destroy the city and the sanctuary; and the end thereof shall be with a flood, and unto the end of the war desolations are determined." We know that Rome is "the people of the prince" who destroyed the sanctuary. The Arab nations surrounding Israel, coupled with the European Union, are two major power blocs that will play a significant endtime role. The rest of the world is identified as "all the earth" or "the Gentiles."

What is the intention of the nations?

The nations of the world are ruled by the god of this world and directly oppose God's plan. This is clearly expressed in Psalm 2:1–2: "Why do the heathen rage, and the people imagine a vain thing? The kings of the earth set themselves, and the rulers take counsel together, against the LORD, and against his anointed...." What are they raging about? What vain thing do they imagine? Verse 3 identifies their goal: "Let us break their bands asunder, and cast away their cords from us." Their rage is directed against the fundamentals of God's law. It is His law that identifies sin. Therefore, it is only natural for the nations to try and change God's law.

Today, many actions that God considers sin have been redefined as "character deficiencies" or "mistakes," or

94

they have been diagnosed as "sickness." One of the most fundamental laws in human history is God's institution of marriage. Today, many married couples are breaking the covenant they made before God and men, and that with the blessing of their church. In order to "avoid" the troubles that sometimes occur in marriage, an increasing number of couples are choosing to live together. Society no longer refers to this as sin, but considers it to be "normal" behavior.

The heathen nations view the law as bondage; they desire to break the bands of the law and cast away the cords that bind them to the God of creation.

How does God react to man's rebellion? "He that sitteth in the heavens shall laugh: the Lord shall have them in derision" (verse 4). That's a relief, at least God is not alarmed. He doesn't take the nations as seriously as we do; He simply laughs at these mere mortals who think they can rebel against Him and get away with it.

But then He gives the answer to all the problems revealed in verse 6: "Yet have I set my king upon my holy hill of Zion." Therefore, the answer to this complexity of the nations lies in Zion, the little place in the land of Israel, in the city of Jerusalem. Mount Moriah is on the extension of Mount Zion where the holy Temple once stood and countless animals were sacrificed to cover the sins of the children of Israel. A little further outside the walls of Jerusalem was a little hill called Calvary. It was there that God allowed sinful man to crucify His only beloved Son. It was there that God reconciled sinful man to Himself. He didn't do it by means of a powerful heavenly host, but by a simple demonstration of humility. Jesus allowed sinful man to take His life. As a result, Satan, the great conspirator against God, committed the biggest mistake ever: For the first time in history, he caused the death of a sinless person. From there, salvation, the gift of eternal life, became available to whoever believes on the name of the Lord Jesus Christ.

That is one reason the nations must oppose Jerusalem. Remember, all nations are under the devil's jurisdiction. Why? Because he who sins is of the devil, and since all have sinned, all have become servants of Satan, Zion's greatest enemy.

What does God think about the nations of the world?

The most simple answer is found in Isaiah 40:17, "All nations before him are as nothing; and they are counted to him less than nothing, and vanity." Therefore, the nations are insignificant as far as God is concerned. That, however, does not mean that God does not care about the nations. When it comes to salvation, the Bible clearly declares that "...God so loved the world, that he gave his only begotten Son, that whosoever believeth in him should not perish, but have everlasting life" (John 3:16). The Bible also makes it clear that God wants all men to be saved and come to know Him. The problem is that each nation thinks too highly of itself. Some think they rule the world, but that is only wishful thinking because ultimately the Creator of heaven and earth is in charge. In the end, it is He, not the political system, who thrones and dethrones.

Generally, the Bible's use of the term "the nations" means all those opposing Israel. That is the only nation God identifies with. He refers to the people of Israel as His people. He refers to Israel as His land, and He has called Jerusalem "the city of peace." It is significant that not one nation agrees that Israel has the legal and biblical right to the land as defined by the God-ordained borders of the Euphrates River and the River of Egypt. To make such a claim is laughable to the nations. Why? Because it is virtually impossible to remove such nations as Lebanon, Syria and Jordan and establish biblical borders. This is out of the question; no sensible and serious-thinking politician would even entertain such a thought. Thus, we see the world becoming perfectly united when it comes to Israel. In view of that fact, God declares that the nations "...are counted to him less than nothing, and vanity."

 ## Why is Rome so significant?

 Of the four Gentile world empires, Rome represents the final Gentile superpower. Israel was under Roman rule when Jesus was born and when He was crucified. According to the prophetic Word, Jesus will return when Rome regains its power over the world. This does not mean that the geo-graphical city located in Italy will literally rule the world, but rather that the Roman system of democracy, free enterprise and freedom of religion will govern the world.

Daniel identified the four Gentile superpowers. He told King Nebuchadnezzar: "...thou art this head of gold." Then he used only a few words to describe the second and third Gentile superpower in Daniel 2:39: "And after thee shall arise another kingdom inferior to thee, and another third kingdom of brass, which shall bear rule over all the earth." Finally, he described the last power structure: "And the fourth kingdom shall be strong as iron: forasmuch as iron breaketh in pieces and subdueth all things: and as iron that breaketh all these, shall it break in pieces and bruise"(verse 40). We know from history that Rome conquered nation after nation using irresistible power in order to subdue all things. Again, this is not limited to the Italian city; it is of global proportion. The Bible says, "...which shall bear rule over all the earth."

Will Rome be the capital of the New World Order?

First, we must understand that Rome plays a much greater role than just being the capital city of Italy. The Roman system dominates four of the world's five continents. Europe, Africa, America and Australia can be considered as predominantly European. The languages are European and their constitutions, systems of law and business practices are all based on Roman laws.

But the Asian continent also depends upon European philosophies and laws. Asian nations are likely to use a European language to communicate with each other. The implementation of laws and conducting of businesses are firmly grounded on Roman principles as well.

Ancient Rome brought the highest glory to Europe. And Europe is the only continent that has permanently molded the nations of the world. The Africans did not establish colonies in America, nor did the Asians do so in Africa, but the Europeans, which we can rightfully call Romans, colonialized almost the entire world.

The July 1997 issue of *National Geographic* published an interesting article on Rome. We quote:

Roman Origins

"We know that early on, the Romans were ruled by the Etruscans, a powerful nation of central Italy. Chafing under an often brutal monarchy, the leading families of Rome finally overthrew the Etruscan kings – a revolution that would influence, some 2,200 years later, the thinking of Thomas Jefferson and George Washington.

"In the year 244 AUC (that is, 509 B.C.) the patrician families of Rome set up a quasi-representative form of government, with a pair of ruling consuls elected for a one-year term. This marked the beginning of the Roman Republic, a form of government that would continue until Julius Caesar crossed the Rubicon 460 years later. Those five centuries were marked by increasing prosperity and increasing democracy."

Rights and Duties of Citizens

"Within the broad sweep of uniformity, Roman administration at the local level was flexible, tolerant, and open.

"When Rome conquered a new province, the defeated general and his army were carted away in chains; almost everyone else came out ahead. The local elite were given positions in the Roman hierarchy. Local businesses gained the benefit of Roman roads, water systems, the laws of commerce and the courts. Roman soldiers guarded the town against pirates and marauders. And within a fairly short period, many of the provincial residents would be made *cives Romani* – citizens of Rome – with all the commensurate rights and duties."

Literacy and Law

"The ideal of written law as a shield – to protect individuals against one another and against the awesome power of the state – was a concept the Romans took from the Greeks. But it was Rome that put this abstract notion into daily practice, and the practice is today honored around the world."

Rome – U.S.A.

"The Roman process of making laws also had

a deep influence on the American system. During the era of the Roman Republic (509 to 49 B.C.) lawmaking was a bicameral activity. Legislation was first passed by the *comitia*, the assembly of the citizens, then approved by the representative of the upper class, the senate, and issued in the name of the senate and the people of Rome. Centuries later, when the American Founding Fathers launched their bold experiment in democratic government, they took republican Rome as their model. Our laws, too, must go through two legislative bodies. The House of Representatives is our assembly of citizens, and, like its counterpart in ancient Rome, the U.S. Senate was originally designed as a chamber for the elite (it was not until the 17th Amendment, in 1913, that ordinary people were allowed to vote for their senators)."

When we understand from Daniel 2 that the fourth kingdom shall subdue all things, and we compare it factually with Roman influence, we see the great significance of the Roman system.

Will Rome be the capital of Europe?

A capital city will not be required in the new developing global society because individual nations will retain their sovereignty, but they will become subject to the systematic authority coined by the New World Order, or whatever its ultimate name may be. The European Union does not need a capital city because each member nation will retain its own identity. Presently, the official European Union governing offices function in Brussels, Belgium and Strasbourg, France. Neither is more important than the other. Both locations serve as a physical address for the bureaucracy of the Union. For example, continuous dialogue goes on among the industrial nations at any given time, but at least once a year, a meeting of the heads of states is scheduled in another city and in another part of the world. These leaders don't need a capital city to meet. But the source and the root of globalism originate with Rome. The European Union, the most powerful economic system in the world, is built on the Treaty of Rome.

T H E N E W
W O R L D
O R D E R

 How new is the New World Order?
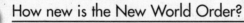

Actually it isn't very new at all. The declaration of the New World Order is documented in Genesis 11:4: "...they said, Go to, let us build us a city and a tower, whose top may reach unto heaven; and let us make us a name, lest we be scattered abroad upon the face of the whole earth." The spirit of the Babel New World Order desired unity, not diversity.

How did God react to this ambition? "Go to, let us go

down, and there confound their language, that they may not understand one another's speech" (Genesis 11:7). As a result, "...the LORD scattered them abroad from thence upon the face of all the earth: and they left off to build the city" (Genesis 11:8).

Today, the spirit of the New World Order is no longer based upon such unity, but is founded upon diversity. For example, the European Union specifically points out that all member nations will be permitted to practice its culture, tradition and language. That is unity through diversity.

 ## Will the New World Order replace a nation's sovereignty?

The New World Order is not an institution, but a definition of global activity and its respective philosophy, expressing new goals and intentions. Sovereign nations will continue to exist. How do we know? The Bible says that the nations will be judged in accordance with their relationship to Israel. National representatives will come to Jerusalem in the 1,000-year kingdom of peace.

Meanwhile, all nations will become dependent upon the New World Order. The Bible makes it clear that a world government will be established.

Therefore, it is a mistake to assume that the New World Order is exclusively expressed through the United Nations, the Trilateral Commission, the Bilderbergers, the Club of Rome or the European Union. The New World Order can best be defined as a progressive, spiritual movement to establish unity among the nations through diversity in the endtimes.

 ### How does the New World Order relate to the United Nations?

 The United Nations is a result of the spirit of the New World Order. The League of Nations was established at the end of World War I. The United Nations was established after World War II, but each had the same goal in mind: uniting the nations to prevent conflict and war and, if possible, punish those who oppose its democratic implementation. This has become increasingly evident in recent years with nations such as

Iraq, Libya, Iran, Cuba, North Korea and others. They are greatly disadvantaged because they do not follow in the footsteps of the spirit of the New World Order. The New World Order promotes the United Nations just like the false prophet will support and promote the agenda of the Antichrist.

Who rules the United Nations?

The spirit of democracy. The United Nations and its many associated institutions will continue to develop and prosper based on the desire of the majority of member nations. Even the Vatican, a religious institution, is a respected member of the United Nations.

At this time, one of the United Nations' most serious deficiencies is finance and military power. No mechanism exists to force member nations to comply with the decision of the majority. The United States particularly acts independent of decisions made by the United Nations. But the Bible says that all nations will come under one umbrella, and we know that sooner or later the United States will also have to submit to the dictates of world democracy.

THE EUROPEAN UNION

 What's so important about the European Union?

 The European Union represents the largest and most diverse economy of the world. The formation of this bloc, based on the Treaty of Rome, is developing into an unprecedented global power bloc. The most important aspect of the European Union is that it is based on diversity. Virtually all other movements and political identities have had one goal – to unify diversity. This is particularly evident in new countries like the United States, which is a nation made up primarily of Europeans from diverse backgrounds with different cultures, traditions and languages. The first thing that was expected from a newcomer was that he or she become an American. His culture, custom, tradition and language were sacrificed on the altar of unity. But look at the wonderful success that resulted. No one can deny that America has shown the world that a diverse people can unite under one political entity and create an equal, and in some cases, better, society than almost any other in the world.

When Daniel spoke of the four Gentile superpowers, he repeatedly emphasized the word "diverse." Daniel 7:23 says, "...The fourth beast shall be the fourth kingdom upon earth, which shall be diverse from all kingdoms, and shall devour the whole earth, and shall tread it down, and break it in pieces."

The diversity consists of the European Union going the opposite way of the new countries. The Union supports, protects and encourages each nation's unique culture, language and identity. Yet, in the end, all of the nations are expected to function as one.

This should not surprise us because the last Gentile super-power "...shall devour the whole earth." What does that mean? We have already answered that question to a degree: Europe, at one time or another, literally dominated the entire world. But here we are speaking about the future. Thus, devouring the whole earth means that the European (Roman) system will be the practicing, political, economic, financial, military and religious philosophy acceptable to the whole world.

 ### What is the difference between the United States of America and the European Union?

 Let's look at the contrast between the United States and Europe. Americans pride themselves on doing everything "the American way." This works extremely well in the United States of America, but it has failed to make converts in other parts of the world. In fact, there are more signs of anti-Americanism throughout the world today than ever before. Why? Because people want to retain their own uniqueness, cultures, traditions and languages.

That's where Europe comes in: Europeans speak about 30 different languages, they are naturally the ones to accommodate other people, other languages, cultures, etc.

We must also keep in mind that at one time or another, most Europeans had colonies in other parts of the world. Naturally, that means they can communicate easier with the rest of the world than Americans can. While the United States' power structure is built on the edict, "United we stand, divided we fall," meaning that all must become equal, the Union's philosophy is based on the principle that all nations should retain their own identity, tradition, culture and especially their languages. We may say "separated we stand but united we think." In short, this is unity through diversity.

 ## Will the European Union fulfill Daniel 7:24?

 Turkey has tried unsuccessfully to become a member of the European Union. France particularly opposes Turkey's membership because the French president said: "Turkey is not Europe, how can they be members of the European Union?" Well said! But, if the Union remains European, then how will this system devour the entire earth? Therefore, it seems only natural that the Mediterranean countries will also be permitted to become members of the Union. It isn't impossible that the Union would change its name from European Union to, perhaps, Global Union.

Many have taken it upon themselves to identify the European Common Market as the final fulfillment of Daniel 7:24, emphasizing ten nations representing the "ten horns" and the "ten kings." We warned against this interpretation back in the '60s: "Let us not look for ten countries being members of the European Common Market constituting the fulfillment of Revelation 17:12. Rather we must look for ten power structures that will develop through the European initiative but will be worldwide" (*How Democracy Will Elect The Antichrist*, page 168).

Meanwhile, the Common Market has become the

European Union, and at this time we do not know what it will be called in the future.

This power bloc is no doubt the head of all the nations of the world, not as a ruler, but as a force of influence. Only Europe has influenced the entire world with its languages, laws, cultures and business practices. The ten kings and ten horns represent ten different global political-economic power structures. But Rome is the permanent and final authority of Gentile power.

 ## Will the European Union be limited to Europe?

 Initially, the European Union will be limited to the continent. However, Europe must ultimately reach outside of its borders. For example, we already mentioned Turkey, an Asian country, that has tried unsuccessfully to gain acceptance into the European Union. The country's leaders are working very hard to qualify for membership and will be accepted sooner or later. Most Mediterranean countries are potential candidates for Union membership although they are not part of the European continent.

It is interesting that the ancient Roman Empire ruled all of the Mediterranean countries from the tip of northern Africa to the Indian Ocean. In the end, however, the world will participate in Europe's success. The Bible says: "Thus he said, The fourth beast shall be the fourth kingdom upon earth, which shall be diverse from all kingdoms, and shall devour the whole earth, and shall tread it down, and break it in pieces" (Daniel 7:23).

 ## Will the European Union become the United States of Europe?

 The distinction between the European Union and the United States of America is based on geographic realities. The United States has little power outside of its borders. Why? Because the United States represents one system, one culture and one language. The European Union reaches far beyond its borders. Its influence may not be recognized by most people at this point. This is partially because each country has its own leader. No one has yet emerged as the ultimate leader of this diverse group of people. Each nation continues to be sovereign, with its own power structure, military operation, government, customs, culture and tradition. However, parallel to each government, there is a shadow government located in the city of Brussels from where laws are being legislated and will ultimately be enforced.

Today, there are 15 voices from 15 individual nations, and 15 representatives from the 15 nations at the European government. Since 2004, there are 25 nations in the Union. In contrast, the United States is one. However, neither the United States nor the European Union can develop independently. Each depends upon the other. This becomes more and more pronounced each time a major industry merger is announced. Permission must be granted by the European Union, the United States and finally the World Trade Organization. A nation's total independence no longer exists.

Can we expect the European Union to be the last world empire?

Definitely! No other political, economic or financial power bloc can match its age, influence and strength. The European Union Treaty is based on irreversible membership; in other words, once a member, always a member.

Above and beyond these facts is the authoritative voice of Scripture. We read about the image of the ages, a statue made out of gold, silver, brass, iron and his feet mixed with iron and clay in Daniel's second chapter. The last power structure is a mixture of iron and clay. That means Roman global laws and the Jewish people, who are represented by clay. This is in the works today. Israel will also become a member of the European Union and for the first time in history will be in danger of losing its identity, which God will not allow. At the end of this global world power structure, God will establish an eternal kingdom. "And in the days of these kings shall the God of heaven set up a kingdom, which shall never be destroyed: and the kingdom shall not be left to other people, but it shall break in pieces and consume all these kingdoms, and it shall stand for ever" (Daniel 2:44).

 The European Union is not the world, so how can it be considered global?

Influence is the key to world dominion. We already mentioned that Union members retain such uniqueness, but they represent a unity by means of diversity.

How can you be unified and diverse at the same time? This appears to be a blatant contradiction, but when we study it carefully, we realize it is not. Take a look at the business world. Large global corporations do not own, manufacture or deal in one product alone; they are diversified. For instance, a telephone company may be part of a food distribution chain or a production firm. Large car manufacturers have a variety of interests in virtually all major branches of the economy. But these big companies are united; they have one board of directors that rules the diverse financial and commercial empire.

That is a picture of Europe today: unity in diversity. The European Union actually has the enforcing power to protect the sovereign identity of all nations while simultaneously welding them together as an irreversible member.

 ## Who is actually in charge of the European Union?

 Again, the answer is democracy. European Union constituents will be molded into a united people becoming economically dependent on each other and working for the common good of all its member nations and citizens. Satan is the one who is really in charge. Needless to say, this is not limited to the European Union, but it includes every nation of the world.

This is revealed to us in Satan's attempt to tempt Jesus by showing Him "...all the kingdoms of the world and the glory of them." Then the devil challenged Jesus: "All these things will I give thee if thou wilt fall down and worship me" (Matthew 4:9). This verse of Scripture seems difficult for nationalists to grasp, particularly those who are fanatically attached to their nation. But we must face the irreversible truth of Scripture: the world is ruled by the father of lies, the originator of sin. Because all nations, and for that matter, all people, are sinful and therefore subject to Satan.

The Bible makes it clear that there are two groups of people: Those who are saved and those who are lost. Second Corinthians 4:4 says: "In whom the god of this world hath blinded the minds of them which believe not." All unbelievers belong to this category; they are subject to the god of this world regardless of what religion they may be following.

Therefore, when we ask who is in charge of the European Union, we shouldn't be surprised that it is the same prince of darkness who is also in charge of the United States or any other country.

How is it possible for the devil to rule the world? The answer is almost too simple. He who sins is of the devil and since "...all have sinned and come short of the glory of God," all have become legally subject

120

to the dictates of the great deceiver.

Israel is the only national exception through which God will establish peace on earth, and through whom He has already established true and eternal peace for all who have put their trust in Jesus.

10

THE UNITED STATES OF AMERICA

 Can the United States of America be found in Bible prophecy?

 It cannot be found as a national identity. America is a nation based upon European culture. The founding fathers were Europeans. Those who drew up the Declaration of Independence were primarily Freemasons and deists. Their main principles were obviously built upon the existing European principles, which are built upon Roman laws and orders. Therefore, America can be found in Bible prophecy, but only as an extension of Europe.

What is the main purpose America has fulfilled?

 The United States of America is the first successful New World Order country. The majority of American citizens forged a unified nation from diverse European nationals. They sacrificed their heritage in order to become integrated into a new vibrant nation that dominated the 1900s as the world's leading power structure.

It is from the United States that the European Union learned how to build a unified power structure from among a group of diverse people. America was prospering while the Europeans were fighting with each other. America has been a pioneer in creating an integrated world.

 ## Will America become an atheistic country?

No! Atheism lost its major influence with the fall of communism. The future of the world is guided by religion; therefore, America will play an integral role by contributing knowledge and experience for the coming religious global power structure. Religion will take a prominent place, as is evident from Revelation 9:20: "And the rest of the men which were not killed by these plagues yet repented not of the works of their hands, that they should not worship devils, and idols of gold, and silver, and brass, and stone, and of wood: which neither can see, nor hear, nor walk." That is about as religious as you can get.

You don't need much of an imagination to see that today's modern world is worshipping what it has created. As the years go by, man will create even more fascinating things so that everyone can enjoy freedom, prosperity and security. Equality must be established between the political structure and religion, which will form the world church.

What does the future hold for America?

America's future is the same as the future of any other nation. According to the prophetic Word, which describes the Antichrist's intent, we are to expect unprecedented peace and prosperity. However, the ultimate end will be the judgment of all nations when Jesus returns and stands on the Mount of Olives. Then Jerusalem will become the capital city of the world. The law will go out from Jerusalem and not one nation will be able to rebel against the authority issued from there.

CHAPTER 11

GLOBALISM

 ## What is globalism?

Globalism can be defined as an activity to unify communication, transportation, commerce, finance and religion. Not only has globalism become popular, but it has become essential. A corporation must become global to ensure its future. No country is big enough to exist on its own merits any longer. Interdependency has progressed to such an extent that even a small disturbance can affect the entire world. Not only did the 1980s stock market crash in Hong Kong affect Asia, but it also took the rest of the world many years to recover. The world has not been the same since the early '90s when West Germany literally bought East Germany. Therefore, what one country does affects the others as well.

 ## When did globalism begin?

Although modern globalism became a reality after World War II, it can be traced back to as early as the Tower of Babel. Genesis 11:2–4 says: "And it came to pass, as they journeyed from the east, that they found a plain in the land of Shinar; and they dwelt there. And they said one to another, Go to, let us make brick, and burn them throughly. And they had brick for stone, and slime had they for mortar. And they said, Go to, let us build us a city and a tower, whose top may reach unto heaven; and let us make us a name, lest we be scattered abroad upon the face of the whole earth." It's striking that the pronouns "we" and "us" are used instead of names. That was democracy in action; the people were in charge, they decided their future and they sought to create a unified world. The people clearly expressed their intention to build a tower that would reach heaven. Should we assume that these people were so primitive to think that they could actually reach heaven? I don't think so. Their sophistication was proven by the grand scale they had for their world at that time. But what it does express is that they wanted to create their own means of salvation. In other words, instead of heaven reaching down to earth toward man, they strove to reach heaven. The Bible teaches that God came down from heaven and became man, not that man goes into heaven to become God.

Two important issues in this passage require closer examination:

1) They had "brick for stone."

A stone is a unique piece of material, just as our fingerprints are so unique that there is no duplicate among the world's six billion people. So why bricks? A brick is made uniformly, each being the same size, weight and form. This teaches us that world unity can be achieved through uniformity. All must become equal. A person's individuality must be done away with.

2) They had "slime for mortar."

This is unusual because mortar is a mixture of lime, sand and water and is readily available in abundance virtually anywhere. Mortar, which holds stones and bricks together, usually consists of a weaker substance. For example, if a wall needed to be torn down, it can be done if the mortar was somewhat weaker than the stones or bricks. This accommodates possible changes such as renovations and alterations. However, in the case of the Tower of Babel, they used "slime" which, translated from the Hebrew, means bitumen, a substance derived from oil.

We all know that the Mideast is the oil barrel of the world. The region controls the flow of oil and can, to a certain degree, dictate the world's energy supply. When these uniform bricks are put together with bitumen, they become stuck to each other inseparably. Crude oil is the substance that unites the world's industry. Since those early days of the building of the Tower of Babel, man has continued to dream of a unified world where peace, security and prosperity exist.

 Will globalism create new laws and orders?

 Psalm 2:1–3 says: "Why do the heathen rage, and

the people imagine a vain thing? The kings of the earth set themselves, and the rulers take counsel together, against the LORD, and against his anointed, saying, Let us break their bands asunder, and cast away their cords from us." What does this passage of Scripture mean? It means that the nations of the world have expressed a desire to live independently from God's law and order. Their aim is to create their own millennium of peace.

Scripture's mention of breaking the cords and casting them away refers to the fundamental laws that God has ordained for mankind. This does not depend upon Christianity alone, but those laws are established throughout the world regardless of religion. Not one country in the world supports murder, rewards liars or encourages thieves. During one of my tours to India, I saw the words: "Government work is God's work" in large letters above a government building in Bangalore.

God-ordained laws and principles are being changed in these endtimes. A drunkard is no longer considered a sinner, he is sick, and in need of help. Homosexuality is an acceptable "alternative lifestyle," not sin, while extramarital affairs have become the norm. In short, globalism is making man "free." However, this freedom is actually a bondage that will ultimately lead to the greatest catastrophe ever.

Who supports globalism?

Democracy is globalism's biggest supporter. Whatever the majority wants, the majority gets. Since the majority of the world's population is evil, it stands to reason that evil will triumph.

The entire world stands behind globalism, and that includes you and me. Let me explain: When you go grocery shopping, you patronize the store that offers the highest quality food at the lowest price. Who can offer that kind of deal? The globalist. You will not get quality at an affordable price at your local "mom and pop" store. That, in simple terms, means you are supporting globalism.

In recent decades, I have noticed that globalism is dictating the prices of many items such as photography, entertainment components and computers. Today, you can buy these items in just about any country for approximately the same price. In summary, globalism offers the

132

consumer the very best at the lowest price. As a result, virtually everybody supports globalism.

 ## Can globalism be stopped?

No! Even those who fight against globalism are actually supporting and promoting it. We already mentioned that greatest value for the least amount of money is offered by the globalist.

In the past, some political candidates have included anti-globalism slogans in their campaign. One advised, "Buy American-made products." A reporter confronted him with the glaring fact that an American product can no longer be properly identified as such. For example, three-quarters of a Japanese car may have been built in the United States, while 60 percent of an American car may have been manufactured in a foreign country. So, which one is American?

Another political candidate tried to garner votes by telling people that if they elected him, he would make sure that no jobs were exported outside of the country. However, just the opposite took place; foreign countries exported jobs to the United States as never before. For example, Europe and Japan invested in the United States more than ever. This is primarily due to an excellent business climate and a work force that is reliable and relatively cheap! It was determined during the late 1990s that four out of every five new jobs in the United States were created by foreign corporations.

CHAPTER
1 2

6 6 6 :
THE MARK
AND TOTAL
CONTROL

 What does the number 666 stand for?

 The number 666 is the number of the Antichrist, who is the epitome of evil.

God worked six days and rested on the seventh. God ordained that man should do likewise.

The number six is what man does; he wants to accomplish his goal of building peace, prosperity and security by himself. Three times six signifies man's work. The Bible says, "Here is wisdom. Let him that hath understanding count the number of the beast: for it is the number of a man; and his number is Six hundred threescore and six" (Revelation 13:18). The Antichrist is the epitome of man's desire and aspiration. He will reflect humanity's hopes and dreams.

Will all people receive the 666 mark?

No! That number is specifically reserved for the Antichrist; however, a number system divided into two categories will be implemented: 1) The name of the beast and 2) The number of his name. Those who receive the name of the beast are the ones most closely associated with him. They will also worship the image of the beast because they are convinced that he is the Christ.

The second group will receive the number of his name. They, too, are in alliance with the Antichrist. They may not be convinced that he is the real Christ; they have accepted the number for practical purposes.

We may compare this with our Social Security numbers. There are no logical reasons for anyone to refuse a newborn baby his Social Security number. While this may have raised plenty of objections a hundred years ago, today, we have grown up with a numbering system and practically all opposition has faded.

Not only do we have Social Security numbers, but there are also many other numbers by which we are identified. To name a few: insurance policies, tax numbers, bank accounts and driver's licenses. You could not exist today if you refused numbers as an identity. However, we must emphasize that the endtime number system will be placed permanently on the right hand or the forehead of every person. That means all the numbers we are identified with today are not the mark of the beast. The name of the beast and the number of his name are still future events.

 ## Can we identify the mark of the beast?

 The Bible explains that the mark of the beast will be placed on the right hand or forehead of an individual. Some people have proposed that the mark of the beast will be a computer chip that is injected underneath a person's skin. This chip is supposed to store significant personal information of an individual. Such a person could literally walk into a shopping mall, make his selection and walk out of the store without any assistance from a salesperson. Sophisticated scanning devices would register the entrance of the person, and the products he selected would be tallied the moment he left. The implanted chip would instantaneously deduct the amount of his purchase from his bank account.

Needless to say, this would stop theft, save money and offer better products at lower prices. In other words, the success of this system will be the key.

However, I am not thoroughly convinced that the chip is the answer. Why? Because that kind of technology is outdated. Computer science is developing at such a pace that whatever is new today may be obsolete tomorrow. We are presently being told that a chip is no longer necessary to identify a person. New computer technology is capable of identifying a person by his appearance, facial contours, weight, height, iris, and even brain waves. The mark of the beast will be the most sophisticated identification system the world has ever seen.

How can we avoid the mark?

Receiving the mark can be avoided by being prepared to receive the alternative, that is, a new name. You will either receive the mark of the beast or "...a new name written, which no man knoweth saving he that receiveth it" (Revelation 2:17). You are either saved or lost; you will either accept Jesus Christ as your personal Savior or you will accept the image of the beast. There is no other way around it. A name is a precious commodity that stays with you all the days of your life. Whenever you hear or read your name, it touches your soul because that name is what identifies you. When you trust Jesus as your Savior, then you have become a new creature. As a result, you will receive a new name after you leave this earth. This name will be created especially for you and it will not be duplicated.

The devil is not capable of creating; the best he can offer is an imitation, and in this case, he can give a number. This reveals how much Satan cares about you; to him you are nothing, you are worthless, you are expressed by a number. This behavior is typical of the father of lies. He seeks to degrade God's creation; unfortunately, he is quite successful.

The overwhelming majority of the world's population gladly, voluntarily and intentionally serves Him. Why? Because they have been deceived. They do not want to hear that they are sinners, never mind have to admit it themselves.

But the Bible says, "All have sinned and come short of the glory of God." That diametrically opposes today's prevailing opinion that each and every soul on the planet is more important than the other. The world believes that there is some good in every person, and that the good will somehow outweigh the bad, therefore, they think they will enter heaven. That is the great lie Satan feeds the multitude.

 ### What happens to those who receive the mark?

 The following five verses reveal what will happen to those who receive the mark:

• "And the smoke of their torment ascendeth up for ever and ever: and they have no rest day nor night, who worship the beast and his image, and whosoever receiveth the mark of his name" (Revelation 14:11).

• "And I saw as it were a sea of glass mingled with fire: and them that had gotten the victory over the beast, and over his image, and over his mark, and over the number of his name, stand on the sea of glass, having the harps of God" (Revelation 15:2).

• "And the first went, and poured out his vial upon the earth; and there fell a noisome and grievous sore upon the men which had the mark of the beast, and upon them which worshipped his image" (Revelation 16:2).

• "And the beast was taken, and with him the false prophet that wrought miracles before him, with which he deceived them that had received the mark of the beast, and them that worshipped his image. These both were cast alive into a lake of fire burning with brimstone" (Revelation 19:20).

• "And I saw thrones, and they sat upon them, and judgment was given unto them: and I saw the souls of them that were beheaded for the witness of Jesus, and for the word of God, and which had not worshipped the beast, neither his image, neither had received his mark upon their foreheads, or in their hands; and they lived and reigned with Christ a thousand years" (Revelation 20:4).

1 3

THE GREAT
TRIBULATION

 What is the Great Tribulation?

 Isaiah described the Great Tribulation in chapter 13:9–11. This is the beginning of God's wrath, which will result in literal darkness, and will be worldwide. Jesus said: "And there shall be signs in the sun, and in the moon, and in the stars; and upon the earth distress of nations, with perplexity; the sea and the waves roaring" (Luke 21:25). In short, the Great Tribulation means the time of grace is over. The climactic reason, however, is what the nations of the world have done with the land of Israel: "I will also gather all nations, and will bring them down into the valley of Jehoshaphat, and will plead with them there for my people and for my heritage Israel, whom they have scattered among the nations, and parted my land" (Joel 3:2). We've mentioned it before; all nations, without exception, are literally parting the land of Israel today. Why? Because they have refused the light of the world, thus their actions are works of darkness.

 ## When will the Great Tribulation begin?

 The Great Tribulation will begin after the Church of Jesus Christ, clearly defined in Scripture as the light of the world, has been removed from the earth. The Great Tribulation is the hour of darkness. The Spirit of God, within the office of the Comforter in the Church, is removed from the world and, as a result, there is great tribulation because there is no light. Jesus said: "For then shall be great tribulation, such as was not since the beginning of the world to this time, no, nor ever shall be" (Matthew 24:21).

Can people be converted during the Great Tribulation?

 Yes, conversions will take place during the Great Tribulation as confirmed by Revelation 7:9: "After this I beheld, and, lo, a great multitude, which no man could number, of all nations, and kindreds, and people, and tongues, stood before the throne, and before the Lamb, clothed with white robes, and palms in their hands." However, these people do not belong to the Church of Jesus Christ. Notice their position and location: "Therefore are they before the throne of God, and serve him day and night in his temple: and he that sitteth on the throne shall dwell among them" (Revelation 7:15). But the Church's position and location is described in Revelation 21:22: "And I saw no temple therein: for the Lord God Almighty and the Lamb are the temple of it."

How is it possible for people to be saved when the Holy Spirit has been removed? The Holy Spirit is removed as the Comforter for the Church, but the Holy Spirit is God, therefore omnipresent. A multitude of people will come to faith in the saving knowledge of the Lord

Jesus Christ and trust Him for their salvation during the Great Tribulation.

 ## Who are the 144,000?

The 144,000 are representatives of the 12 tribes of Israel. The Bible makes it clear that 12,000 from each tribe will be sealed so that they will be able to proclaim the truth to the world after the Church has been removed. Severe persecution of the Jews will result in response to their testimony. These 144,000 are called "...the servants of our God." In chapter 14, we see the 144,000 in the presence of the Lamb on Mount Zion and verse 4 clearly states, "These are they which were not defiled with women, for they are virgins...." What does this mean? They have not participated in the great global fornication of the success of "Mystery Babylon the great, the mother of harlots and abomination of the earth" (Revelation 17:5). Revelation 18:3 says: "...all nations have drunk of the wine of the wrath of her fornication...." These 144,000 were not polluted with the horrible sins of fornication instituted by Mystery Babylon. They heeded the voice, "...Come out of her, my people, that ye be not partakers of her sins, and that ye receive not of her plagues" (Revelation 18:4).

 ## What is the calling of the 144,000?

 The calling of the 144,000 is to testify to the world that Jesus is the Messiah. The world will become intoxicated by an unprecedented success of peace and prosperity during the Great Tribulation. The one global religion will glorify man, which constitutes spiritual fornication. Scripture makes it apparent that these 144,000 will have abstained from such activity. How they achieve it is through the blood of the Lamb. It is also safe to say that they will not participate in the global political religious fornication as well. Notice they are "...the firstfruits unto God and to the land," which corresponds with Romans 11:16, "For if the firstfruit be holy, the lump is also holy: and if the root be holy, so are the branches."

How long will the Great Tribulation last?

Scripture says that the Great Tribulation will last for seven years. The first three-and-a-half years will be characterized by the success of the Antichrist and his New World Order. In the midst of those seven years, during which the Temple in Jerusalem will be rebuilt, the Antichrist will demand that the sacrifices cease. He then will sit in the Temple and declare himself to be God.

Daniel documents the time period of the Antichrist: "And he shall confirm the covenant with many for one week: and in the midst of the week he shall cause the sacrifice and the oblation to cease, and for the overspreading of abominations he shall make it desolate, even until the consummation, and that determined shall be poured upon the desolate" (Daniel 9:27).

During these days of the Great Tribulation, the time will come when the Jews recognize that the Antichrist is not the Messiah, but an imposter. Israel will cry out to God, and He will answer: "And I will pour upon the house of David, and upon the inhabitants of Jerusalem, the spirit of grace and of supplications: and they shall look upon me whom they have pierced, and they shall mourn for him, as one mourneth for his only son, and shall be in bitterness for him, as one that is in bitterness for his firstborn" (Zechariah 12:10).

What is the ministry of the two witnesses?

The two witnesses will have special authority by God to testify to the truths in the city of Jerusalem. Their names are not mentioned; therefore, their identity is open to speculation. Some people believe they are Moses and Elijah, while others think they are Elijah and Enoch. The latter identification is based on the fact that these two men were raptured and did not taste death, because the Bible says that it is appointed for man once to die. However, I believe that the two witnesses are Moses and Elijah. Moses and Elijah appeared with Jesus on the Mount of Transfiguration. God gave Moses the power to turn water into blood. Elijah called down fire from heaven and shut the heavens so that it would not rain. Moses represents the law; Elijah represents judgment. While Moses did actually die, his death occurred outside of the Promised Land, and it was not the result of sin or physical deterioration. The Bible testifies, "...his eye was not dim, nor his natural force abated" (Deuteronomy 34:7). God took Moses' life and the Lord Himself buried him.

I also believe the two witnesses are Moses and Elijah because of the Lord's statement that a prophet cannot die outside of Jerusalem. Therefore, these two prophets will have to come to Jerusalem, die there and, after three days, resurrect and ascend into heaven.

 ## Who are the two witnesses of Revelation 11?

They are the two "olive branches" (Zechariah 4:12), witnesses sent for the sake of the Jews and the world after the Church has been removed. God did not ordain two avenues of salvation to take place on earth simultaneously, so the Church cannot be here during that time. The Old Testament ordination ended with Jesus' crucifixion, which is clearly illustrated by the abolition of the Temple service the moment Jesus died when the curtain in the Holy of Holies was torn from top to bottom.

The two witnesses appear before the seventh angel sounds the trumpet of judgment. The world at that time will be in a terrible shape due to the Antichrist's deception. Revelation 9:20–21 says: "And the rest of the men which were not killed by these plagues yet repented not of the works of their hands, that they should not worship devils, and idols of gold, and silver, and brass, and stone, and of wood: which neither can see, nor hear, nor walk: Neither repented they of their murders, nor of their sorceries, nor of their fornication, nor of their thefts." In other words, the world will be given over to idolatry. The Church will be gone, and with it, the light will be gone as well. Darkness will prevail as the world follows the system of Antichrist. But because God never leaves the world without a testimony, these two witnesses appear with a message that exposes the Antichrist's lies.

How does the world react to the testimony of the two witnesses?

After demonstrating God's power to the people in Jerusalem and the world, "...when they shall have finished their testimony, the beast that ascendeth out of the bottomless pit shall make war against them, and shall overcome them, and kill them" (Revelation 11:7), a global Christmas party will begin: "And they that dwell upon the earth shall rejoice over them, and make merry, and shall send gifts one to another; because these two prophets tormented them that dwelt on the earth" (verse 10).

How will the two witnesses torment the people on earth? By proclaiming the truth. But as we already mentioned, they are the reason it doesn't rain and the water turns into blood. Plus, they will have power over plagues upon the earth to punish mankind.

Their bodies will lie in the streets of Jerusalem, but they will arise from death after three days, and will be seen by the people in Jerusalem. Then they will hear the voice of God say: "...come up hither." As a result, we read in verse 13: "...and the remnant were affraighted, and gave glory to the God of heaven." The resurrection and ascension of the two witnesses is the turning point for the Jewish people during the Great Tribulation.

CHAPTER 14

REVELATION
EVENTS

Who is the Bride of the Lamb?

The Church of Jesus Christ is the Bride of the
Lamb. We belong to Him! He is the Head and we
are His Body. This is the most intimate group of believers
closest to the Bridegroom. However, we must not confuse
this position with our earthly understanding of the bridegroom and bride. Such relations do not exist in heaven, but
serve as an illustration for us to demonstrate the intimacy
and closeness we will be privileged to experience for all
eternity with the Lord Jesus Christ who loved us and re-
deemed us from the powers of darkness with His own pre-

cious blood. The Apostle Paul reveals the Bride in 2nd Corinthians 11:2: "For I am jealous over you with godly jealousy: for I have espoused you to one husband, that I may present you as a chaste virgin to Christ." Revelation 21:2 says: "And I John saw the holy city, new Jerusalem, coming down from God out of heaven, prepared as a bride adorned for her husband."

 ### Why will the leaves of the Tree of Life heal the nations?

 The Tree of Life will serve as a memorial or remembrance of what Jesus has done. In the same way we take the Lord's Supper to remember His death and what He has done for us, so too will the nations that have been healed from their deception be able to partake of the leaves as a memorial to what has been done for them. In other words, the nations will not be healed by the leaves of the Tree of Life but because they are healed they will become partakers of the leaves of the Tree of Life.

Who is Gog and Magog of Ezekiel 38 and 39 and Revelation 20?

Geographic references from Ezekiel 38 and 39 identify an enemy in the uttermost part of Israel. It also adds five allied nations: Persia, Ethiopia, Libya, Gomer and Togarmah. The Gog and Magog mentioned in Revelation chapter 20 are not related to the Gog and Magog of Ezekiel. Why not? Because the Bible says, "...they went up on the breadth of the earth...." In other words they ascended from out of the earth. Then "...fire came down from God out of heaven, and devoured them" (Revelation 20:9b). There is no evidence of bodies, war materials or any weapons. The Gog and Magog of Ezekiel result in countless bodies that will have to be buried. An abundance of war equipment will be used for fuel over the next seven years. The Ezekiel event is motivated by material gain. The Revelation event is aimed against Jerusalem. But nothing is listed of that kind in the Gog and Magog rebellion of Revelation 20. In both cases Gog and Magog are an expression of "anti-God," not Antichrist.

Will literal Babylon be rebuilt?

 No! Judgment upon Babylon was executed some 2,500 years ago. The prophet Jeremiah mentions Babylon 36 times in chapter 51 and concludes, "And thou shalt say, Thus shall Babylon sink, and shall not rise from the evil that I will bring upon her: and they shall be weary. Thus far are the words of Jeremiah" (verse 64).

Archaeological Babylon is quite fascinating and much of the ruins have been excavated. A few walls were rebuilt during the Saddam Hussein administration, but in the meantime, much of it has been torn down as Iraqis scavenge the bricks for themselves or sell them as souvenirs. The original ancient Babylon is a desolation located in a swamp, thus, verse 29 reads: "And the land shall tremble and sorrow: for every purpose of the LORD shall be performed against Babylon, to make the land of Babylon a desolation without an inhabitant."

 ## Is Rome Mystery Babylon?

In order to qualify for the title of "Mystery Babylon," a four-fold criteria must first be met:

1. The blood of the martyrs of Jesus must be shed in that city. "And I saw the woman drunken with the blood of the saints, and with the blood of the martyrs of Jesus: and when I saw her, I wondered with great admiration" (Revelation 17:6).

2. Topographically, it must be built on seven hills. "And here is the mind which hath wisdom. The seven heads are seven mountains, on which the woman sitteth" (Revelation 17:9).

3. This city must be a spiritual headquarters for globalism, not only in merchandising, but also in politics, philosophy and religion. "For all nations have drunk of the wine of the wrath of her fornication, and the kings of the earth have committed fornication with her, and the merchants of the earth are waxed rich through the abundance of her delicacies" (Revelation 18:3).

4. When the city is on fire, it must be seen from the Mediterranean Sea. No other city can meet this four-fold criteria but Rome.

"For in one hour so great riches is come to nought. And every shipmaster, and all the company in ships, and sailors, and as many as trade by sea, stood afar off, And cried when they saw the smoke of her burning, saying, What city is like unto this great city!" (Revelation 18:17–18).

 ## Who are the ten kings mentioned in Revelation 17:12?

The ten kings mentioned in Revelation 17:12 are identical to the ten horns spoken of in Daniel 7:7. "And the ten horns which thou sawest are ten kings, which have received no kingdom as yet; but receive power as kings one hour with the beast. These have one mind, and shall give their power and strength unto the beast" (Revelation 17:12–13). They do not represent ten European nations, but ten power structures into which the world will be divided. However, Europe will dominate because it has subjected the world to its laws, philosophies and political infrastructure. Therefore, these ten kings represent the entire world which, indeed, will have one mind and will fully cooperate with the final world ruler, the Antichrist.

Can we expect a nuclear war?

Historically speaking, it is safe to say that anything is possible. Every weapon that has ever been manufactured has been used for the express purpose of destroying man. Will nuclear weapons be used? This issue is open to speculation.

However, the description we find in the Bible, particularly in the book of Revelation, is not the cause of a man-made nuclear holocaust. The endtime judgments we read about are unto destruction and they are caused by God, "...men were scorched with great heat, and blasphemed the name of God, which hath power over these plagues: and they repented not to give him glory" (Revelation 16:9). This makes it clear that God, not man, has the power over these plagues. The people "...blasphemed the name of God," which means that they will know that God is the source of their punishment.

Incidentally, this shows how far deception can go. These plagues were the result of the fourth vial of wrath. Then the fifth vial is poured "...upon the seat of the beast and his kingdom...." What is the result? "And blasphemed the God of heaven because of their pains and their sores, and repented not of their deeds" (verse 11).

Who are "they" who will say "peace and safety"?

The word "they" in 1st Thessalonians 5 refers to the people of the world, particularly the Jews. However, we must stress that such a peace will not be forced upon the people, but it will be wholeheartedly endorsed by both Jews and Arabs. That means a spirit of peace will suddenly prevail among the people and that will lead to an unprecedented form of cooperation. However, this spirit of peace is the product of the great deceiver, the father of lies.

Will the world experience peace?

Yes. Why? Because the Bible promises that there will be peace from one end of the earth to the other. Therefore, it stands to reason that the devil, the great imitator of God's work, must produce a global peace that is unprecedented in mankind's history.

This peace will come about through the avenue of deception. The word "deception" already indicates that this is a voluntary matter. Those who have been deceived do not think they are; in fact, they are fully convinced that what is being presented is the absolute truth.

For example, the belief that man is inherently good, and if we could only develop this good, mankind would become good and good would result in peace. This fallacy is globally accepted.

The Bible says there is not an ounce of good in man. As a matter of fact, the Bible states that the heart of man is continuously evil and stresses there is none righteous, not even one. The Apostle Paul confessed of himself, "There is no good in my flesh." Why? Because flesh and blood cannot inherit the kingdom of God. They are corrupt; therefore, the only peace man can produce is a deceptive one.

 If peace is good and is desired by all, why can't it be lasting?

 Because man's idea of peace is built on his own ability to produce it; he never takes his sinful nature into account. Not only is peace the absence of war or conflict, but real lasting peace is based on love. Real peace was introduced when Jesus died on Calvary's cross, pouring out His blood for the sins of mankind. The price for peace was paid in full. Each and every one of us who believes in Jesus as his/her personal Savior becomes a child of peace. In the midst of a world that stands in conflict with one another, incapable of producing a lasting form of peace, the sacrificial love of our Lord is and always will be the answer.

 ## Will a religious peace produce peace?

 Without a doubt, the religious institutions of the world desire peace more than anything else. Dialogues have been developed for many decades among the major and minor religious institutions of the world in an attempt to find common ground. Basically, all religions have the same message: Do good and you will be rewarded for it in heaven, do evil and you will be punished. No religion rewards stealing, lying, murder or adultery. Therefore, it stands to reason that the religions of the world will form a united front and present a constitution for peace on earth. It will be successful, but it will not last.

 ## How can I obtain peace?

This is the most important question anyone will ever ask. All the knowledge in the world cannot surpass him who can say, "I have the peace of God in my heart." The Lord Jesus said: "Peace I leave with you, my peace I give unto you: not as the world giveth, give I unto you. Let not your heart be troubled, neither let it be afraid" (John 14:27). This is extremely significant because Jesus differentiates between the peace of the world and the peace that only comes from Him. Why can He give peace that is better than all others? Because He paid the price for eternal peace when he sacrificed Himself on Calvary's cross for our sins: Peace is not only the absence of war or conflict, but real peace is having the knowledge that our sins have been forgiven, giving us peace with God. When we ask the Lord Jesus for forgiveness, we receive this peace of which the Apostle Paul wrote: "And the peace of God, which passeth all understanding, shall keep your hearts and minds through Christ Jesus" (Philippians 4:7).

THE
MILLENNIUM

 ## What is the Millennium?

 The Millennium is the answer to Jesus' prayer: "Thy kingdom come, thy will be done in earth as it is in heaven." When we read the Old Testament, we notice that the patriarchs, the prophets, the kings and the priests looked forward to this kingdom of peace. The Millennium is also the fulfillment of Psalm 22:27–28: "All the ends of the world shall remember and turn unto the LORD: and all the kindreds of the nations shall worship before thee. For the kingdom is the LORD'S: and he is the governor among the nations."

What is the cause of the Millennium?

 The Millennium is the result of Jesus' victory over Satan: "And he laid hold on the dragon, that old serpent, which is the Devil, and Satan, and bound him a thousand years, And cast him into the bottomless pit, and shut him up, and set a seal upon him, that he should deceive the nations no more, till the thousand years should be fulfilled: and after that he must be loosed a little season" (Revelation 20:2-3). The deceiver will no longer be able to do his work because he will be shut up in the bottomless pit for a thousand years.

 ## Who will take part in the Millennium?

Israel will partake in the Millennium because they are the only nation that has been given a collective promise that will result in their national conversion. The Bible makes it clear that Israel will rule over the nations; therefore, remnants of the nations will also enter the thousand-year kingdom of peace, but they will be ruled with a rod of iron. In other words, sin will not be tolerated. This is evident from Isaiah 65:20: "There shall be no more thence an infant of days, nor an old man that hath not filled his days: for the child shall die an hundred years old; but the sinner being an hundred years old shall be accursed."

Where will the Church be during the Millennium?

First Thessalonians 4:17 makes the church's position clear: "Then we which are alive and remain shall be caught up together with them in the clouds, to meet the Lord in the air: and so shall we ever be with the Lord." Notice the sentence, "...and so shall we ever be with the Lord." In other words, wherever the Lord is, there we shall be also.

Will mortal saints intermingle on earth with the immortal during the Millennium?

There is no evidence in Scripture that the saints who came down from heaven will intermingle with mortal men on earth. The glorified saints have a to-

169

tally different position and task, "And hast made us unto our God kings and priests; and we shall reign on the earth" (Revelation 5:10). Those who will be saved during the Millennium will participate in the first resurrection and will become immortal saints.

What is the last battle according to Scripture?

Revelation 20:7-8 says, "And when the thousand years are expired, Satan shall be loosed out of his prison. And shall go out to deceive the nations which are in the four quarters of the earth, Gog and Magog, to gather them together to battle: the number of whom is as the sand of the sea."

What is the aim of Gog and Magog?

What is their intention? "And they went up on the breadth of the earth, and compassed the camp of the saints about, and the beloved city: and fire came down from God out of heaven, and devoured them" (verse 9). This is the final stand of evil against God and against His holy city. As we can see, this last conflict results in the total elimination of the opposition: "...fire came down from God out of heaven, and devoured them." There are no bodies or weapons left over.

What will happen to the unbeliever after the Millennium?

All who followed the deceiver will be judged: "And I saw the dead, small and great, stand before God; and the books were opened: and another book was opened, which is the book of life: and the dead were judged out of those things which were written in the books, according to their works" (Revelation 20:12). These are those who have died without accepting God's free gift of salvation. They will be judged, but will have no chance of salvation. We read this horrible statement in verses 13–15: "And the sea gave up the dead which were in it; and death and hell delivered up the dead which were in them: and they were judged every man according to their works. And death and hell were cast into the lake of fire. This is the second death. And whosoever was not found written in the Book of Life was cast into the lake of fire."

 ## Can you explain the heavenly Jerusalem?

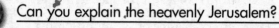

Revelation 21:2,10 says: "And I John saw the holy city, new Jerusalem, coming down from God out of heaven, prepared as a bride adorned for her husband...And he carried me away in the spirit to a great and high mountain, and shewed me that great city, the holy Jerusalem, descending out of heaven from God." The Lamb's wife, the Bride, is veiled in the glory of the heavenly Jerusalem. It is significant that prior to this vision, John is told to, "...Come hither, I will show thee the bride, the Lamb's wife." Yet the Lamb's wife is not actually revealed, we only see the heavenly Jerusalem and its glory. It is also the dwelling place of God with man, "...Behold, the tabernacle of God is with men" (Revelation 21:3).

 ## What will our position be after the Millennium?

"Blessed and holy is he that hath part in the first resurrection: on such the second death hath no

172

power, but they shall be priests of God and of Christ, and shall reign with him a thousand years" (Revelation 20:6). The first resurrection includes all who have been saved; they shall never die.

An indescribable glory awaits those who have accepted Jesus as their personal Savior: "And God shall wipe away all tears from their eyes; and there shall be no more death, neither sorrow, nor crying, neither shall there be any more pain: for the former things are passed away. And he that sat upon the throne said, Behold, I make all things new. And he said unto me, Write: for these words are true and faithful. And he said unto me, It is done. I am Alpha and Omega, the beginning and the end. I will give unto him that is athirst of the fountain of the water of life freely. He that overcometh shall inherit all things; and I will be his God, and he shall be my son" (Revelation 21:4–7). We do not have the ability to imagine what is being prepared for those who love God. Therefore, every believer has a deep desire and longing to be in the presence of the Lord, and thus, the Bible concludes: "He which testifieth these things saith, Surely I come quickly. Amen. Even so, come, Lord Jesus. The grace of our Lord Jesus Christ be with you all. Amen" (Revelation 22:20–21).